THE SECURE BOARD

HOW TO BE CONFIDENT THAT YOUR ORGANISATION IS CYBER SAFE

Anna Leibel   **Claire Pales**

LONGUEVILLE
MEDIA

First published 2021 for Anna Leibel and Claire Pales by

LONGUEVILLE
MEDIA

Longueville Media Pty Ltd
PO Box 205
Haberfield NSW 2045 Australia
www.longmedia.com.au
info@longmedia.com.au
Tel. +61 410 519 685

A CIP catalogue record for this book is available from the National Library of Australia website: www.nla.gov.au

ISBN: 978-0-6489736-7-6

A catalogue record for this book is available from the National Library of Australia

WHAT OTHERS ARE SAYING

"We have seen many significant cyber-attacks and IT failures in recent times, some with spectacular consequences for business and governments. This book is a welcome and timely reminder of our responsibilities (and liability) as board directors. We cannot be IT illiterate or ignorant. Whilst we need not be IT experts, cyber risk must be understood and addressed at the board level. I congratulate Pales and Leibel for this worthy contribution to building our awareness and suggesting practical solutions."

– **Michael Gorton AM,** Lawyer and Board Director; Chair, Alfred Health; Senior Principal, Russell Kennedy Lawyers

"Over the last two decades of working with Claire and Anna on a professional and personal level, I have seen them progress their careers on the world stage, taking calculated risks and roles in a sometimes-difficult industry. They are now recognised as true leaders in the field of information security and risk education for organisations. I am genuinely rapt to see them collaborate on this important and easy-to-understand book. The clear take-aways for readers reflect their style and message, and provide common-sense suggestions using effective examples based on their deep knowledge and experience.

Security risk and the threat of cyber compromise is a very real threat to any organisation. This compilation is a timely, valuable and essential read for anyone seeking out or has a Board appointment. To be provided the opportunity to access the knowledge and experience of these respected industry captains, makes this book an essential read."

– **Darren Kane** has over 20 years' experience in information security-based roles. He was the former Global Corporate Security Director at Telstra and is currently the Chief Security Officer at nbn.

"In the midst of competing demands, cyber security is often deferred. However, like in the event of a major security incident or fraud you may find yourself wishing you had done more.

Pales and Leibel can help. They translate the intangible world of cyber security into familiar standard business and governance practices. They lay out the facts, the business logic and the questions to be asked by all Directors and C-Suite Executives.

If you want to close your performance gap, I recommend spending time with Pales and Leibel. They make it easy to get to grips with cyber security. You won't regret it!"

— **Quinn Pawson**, Chief Executive Officer, VincentCare Victoria

"Cyber security is a critical issue for every director in every sector of the economy. "The Secure Board" is an important contribution to director education and should help all of us to have a better understanding of what cyber risk comprises and what we, as directors, should be concerned about and what we are responsible for. I believe that the title of element 1 helps us remember the significance of the task in front of us: cyber is a business risk, not an IT problem."

— **Peggy O'Neal AO**, Lawyer, President and Board Chairperson

"As the saying goes, we live in interesting times ... and never more when contemplating the reality that global criminal gangs and state sponsors make it their business to disrupt your business. We all spend countless hours at boards thinking about our markets and our competitive responses. How much do we really know about the bigger threat to our business, and how we are planning to protect it? This very well written and researched book is a timely and thoughtful reminder of our obligations as directors and gatekeepers ..."

— **Therese Ryan**, Chair Gippsland Water, Deputy Chair VicForests and Non Executive Director

"A wise read for Board Directors and Business Leaders. Anna and Claire explain the importance of treating Cybersecurity as a key business risk, in a way that is incredibly relatable and easy to understand. This book provides the reader with a foundation to ensure the governance of Cybersecurity risk becomes common boardroom practice."

– **Samm Macleod**, Chief Information Security Officer

"Claire Pales was originally recommended to me to assist with an urgent security recruitment. Reading her first book "The Secure CIO" convinced me Claire could help. Her deep knowledge of cyber security combined with impressive business acumen, an ability to ask probing questions, following up with strategic yet pragmatic advice, solved my crisis and a whole lot more. Claire's guidance enhanced my message to the Board, my peers, and the company generally on the importance of cyber security and that it takes a whole of business approach. Now as a non-executive director, I will be sharing the knowledge contained in this new book with the boardrooms of other organisations, continuing to improve cyber risk management."

– **Michelle Beveridge**, Previously CIO, Intrepid Group

FOREWORD

David Thodey

Every leader is aware of the profound changes that technology has made to how we work and how we do business. Thanks to computing power and the internet, there are massive volumes of data flowing around the world at breathtaking speed. This is both inspiring and concerning for those who are responsible for running and governing corporations.

It is inspiring because technology creates opportunities for businesses to become more efficient and effective. It can also open entirely new markets and expansion prospects.

But it is also concerning because senior executives and directors, now more than ever, need to incorporate the necessary considerations to ensure they're protected against the growing threat from cyber-attacks.

Globally, cybercrime increased by 600 percent in 2020, due largely to COVID-19 changing work practices and rocketing phishing attacks.

Ransomware attacks had a significant impact on Australian organisations across business, the public service and government. Many functions at Toll Group were severely impacted (twice), surgeries were stopped at four hospitals in regional Victoria, Service NSW suffered a serious data breach, and Blue Scope Steel, My Budget and The Australian Wool Exchange also experienced ransomware attacks, just to name a few.

In June 2020, our Prime Minister also announced that government and industry in Australia were being targeted by major cyber-attacks with a significant level of sophistication and capability.

The threat landscape today is extremely complex and sophisticated. We as leaders must meet that level of sophistication by implementing robust information security initiatives for our own organisations.

Data and technology have been ever-present during my career, beginning with when I joined IBM in the late 1970s, and since then I have watched the prominence of information security continue to grow.

While I was CEO of Telstra between 2009 to 2015, we established information security as a part of our company's growth agenda, both as a means to manage our own cyber security and also to provide security products to customers. During that time, Telstra acquired information security and data management company Bridge Point and invested in online contract management company DocuSign.

As Chairman of CSIRO – Australia's national science agency – we have seen cyber security grow into an issue of national and international significance. In response, Data61, the digital innovation arm of CSIRO, was tasked with developing Australia's national cyber security capability as a member of the Cyber Security Cooperative Research Centre.

CSIRO was also a key advisor to the Federal Government's Cyber Security Strategy 2020, which made clear that company directors are responsible for corporate Australia's information security. While executives don't need to be technical experts, they do need to understand they have a legal, fiduciary and potentially also a regulatory obligation to ensure their company's cyber security measures are appropriate.

Businesses also have a significant role to play in our nation's cyber resilience, and it is important that the government and the private sector work together to improve cyber security for our nation. I think we will see the mandatory inclusion of standard cyber security clauses in technology contracts with Australian government departments, and an increased focus on the alignment of cyber security expectations with third parties.

It is imperative that executives and boards accept cyber security as a fundamental issue to their operations, and plan appropriately to mitigate risk.

The Secure Board outlines the critical elements of governing cyber security risks, from strategy and the importance of being prepared, to the role each person in the organisation must play in keeping information safe and secure.

Collectively, Anna and Claire have worked in senior technology and security roles for more than 40 years across Australia and Asia, including several years at Telstra. The Secure Board captures their learnings from the executive to the role of the board, and they clearly explain how to effectively govern cyber risk.

I recommend The Secure Board as essential reading for all leaders. It will equip you with the knowledge and foresight to protect your information and your people.

David Thodey AO
Chair of CSIRO

INTRODUCTION

Ken Lay

As I pondered how I might best contribute to introducing this book, my device notified me of an incoming "media alert". Another story of a data breach. This time in Europe resulting in confidential and highly sensitive personal information being posted by hackers. Fresh in my mind were the recent reports of the unauthorised access to patient medical records in an Australian health service and then last year's ransomware attack that disabled a number of Victorian health service systems for weeks.

Whether in the health sector or elsewhere, these attacks diminish the confidence of the community in the ability of its agencies to secure some of our most sensitive personal information. As a consequence, agency brands are harmed, the reputation and competence of boards and management are questioned, and more importantly, the lives of individuals are disrupted and their privacy is sometimes grievously breached.

Whether in the public or private sector, these stories are no longer unusual or rare. All of us are witnessing the constant attacks on our systems and information. These strikes range from annoying to catastrophic. No matter the impact, the stream of cyber incursions are clear signposts that the governance world has to change quickly. As Directors, we all have a fundamental obligation to understand how best to ensure our organisations are cyber safe.

All contemporary Directors are now on a unending journey to better understand these challenges and to ensure proper oversight of all cyber risks. This will require Directors to self-reflect on their current level of competence. In most cases it will require an investment in education and development. That investment will pay dividends. It will enable Directors to "ask the right questions" and be able to respectfully challenge both Directors and management from an informed position. The benefits are obvious.

The Secure Board is a practical and informative tool to help Directors who are striving to achieve a cyber safe organisation. Whether an experienced Chair or Director, or for someone just starting their governance career, the authors translate their years of experience into a form that is both intelligible and informative. The jargon is set aside, the concepts are simplified and as a result, the complex becomes clearer.

We are invited to take on a "beginners mind" as concepts are developed. This approach resonated with me and I am sure it will challenge you to stop, to reflect and then re-set some of your governance thinking.

What I have learned has made me a better Director. I ask better questions, I better understand consequences of decisions, and ultimately that translates into better Board performance.

Thank you, Anna and Claire, you have made a great contribution to the development of all Directors who choose to pick up this book.

Ken Lay AO APM FAICD
Lieutenant-Governor of Victoria, Board Chairperson
and Director

CONTENTS

THE AUTHORS

Claire Pales is a best selling author, a podcast host and Director of The Security Collective, a consulting company committed to coaching boards, CIOs, and cyber security professionals to help businesses establish exceptional cyber security practices.

She has 17 years of experience establishing teams and leading award-winning security strategies throughout Australia and Asia, including Hong Kong, China, and India.

In addition to a postgraduate qualification in eCrime, Claire is a qualified coach and graduate of the Australian Institute of Company Directors (GAICD). In 2019, Claire was named a Fellow of the Australian Information Security Association (FAISA).

This year, Claire is proud to have become a member of the Technology Committee at the Breast Cancer Network Australia, a cause that is close to her heart. Based in Geelong, Claire is a mum to four children, a sought after speaker and an advocate for all people in cyber.

Anna Leibel is an experienced senior executive across the financial services, management consulting and technology industries. With more than two decades in leadership, Anna is a sought after board advisor on customer and digital transformations, data, cyber, leadership and culture.

Anna's depth of experience in leading technology, strategic project delivery and operations functions with regulated corporates means she has unique insight into governance, risk and compliance, developing business cases for change programs and engaging with executives and board members. In her corporate roles, Anna's motivation is to drive change and innovation that delivers commercial and customer benefits, seeing technology as an enabler to achieve these outcomes.

She is a Non-Executive Director of Ambulance Victoria and a graduate of the Australian Institute of Company Directors. Anna holds a Postgraduate Certificate in IT leadership and has participated in two senior executive programs at Massachusetts Institute of Technology (MIT).

Based in Melbourne, Anna is passionate about bringing more women into leadership. She mentors and encourages our youth to explore careers in STEM and is now sharing her experience as an independent advisor to CEOs and board directors, and as an executive coach.

'Ranked as one of the top ten risks of immediate concern by the World Economic Forum, cyber security is a company-boardroom-level issue.'

– Harvard Law School Reform on Corporate Governance

THAT WAS THEN;
THIS IS NOW

In 1995, The Court of Appeal in the case of Daniels (formerly practising as Deloitte Haskins & Sells) v Anderson (1995) found that the director's duty of care cannot be limited by the director's knowledge, experience, or ignorance and inaction.[1] Instead, directors are required to take reasonable steps to guide and monitor the management of the company.

When this case was heard, it had been 70 years since such a landmark reform had occurred in relation to directors' duties in Australia that would establish the modern-day standard of care and the core irreducible standards for directors. In 1925, board directors were simply required to exhibit the degree of skill that might reasonably be expected of their knowledge and experience. This was the required standard of care of a director demonstrated in the case of *Re City Equitable Fire Insurance Co Ltd*, a UK common law case concerning directors' duties and, in particular, their duty of care.[2]

The James Hardie case came next, in 2001, the findings from which reinforced the standard that directors are held to. By the end of 2019, the Australian Securities & Investments Commission (ASIC) handed down their report on director and officer oversight of non-financial risk. Their corporate governance taskforce and the Financial Services Royal Commission uncovered what happens when proper oversight and management of non-financial risks are not made a priority.

'The evidence before the Commission showed that, too often, boards did not get the right information about emerging non-financial risks; did not do enough to seek further or better information where what they had was clearly deficient; and did not do enough with the information they had to oversee and challenge management's approach to these risks.'[3]

While the broader details of the above rulings are a discussion for another day, what we can say is that these symbolic cases demonstrate that there is no fear in the courts and regulators in holding directors accountable, liable, and to a higher standard than those who have come before.

If you are reading this with your company director 'hat' on, you already know that your role, under the Corporations Act 2001, is to 'act honestly, in good faith and to the best of your ability in the interests of the company'.[4] With the world in a constant state of change, this role is forever becoming more complex.

Even just a few decades ago, directors could never have expected that the internet would, in 2021, be considered a basic human right, be as critical to our survival as food and water, and have the ability to be used for evil even more so than it is used for good.

The internet can start world wars, infect our water systems, and render global giants of industry bankrupt through sheer advances of technology.

Our point is that directors have had to come a long way in just a few short years to uphold their duties. A hockey-stick learning curve for directors has been apparent when it comes to climate change, modern slavery, social media, artificial intelligence, cloud, and the digital transformation of our critical infrastructure. And then there is cyber. A small word that takes in a big definition.

The role of cyber and the board

The Australian Cyber Security Centre (ACSC) defines cyber safety as 'the safe and responsible use of Information and Communication Technologies'.[5] In the same breath, cyber security is considered to be 'measures used to protect the confidentiality, integrity and availability of systems and information'.[6] These technologies and systems run the modern world as we know it. No organisation can claim they are not a technology company, and, therefore, every employee, from new graduates to the board chair, must educate themselves to a level of technical literacy commensurate with the industry, their role, and the expectations of their stakeholders.

While the ACSC may have a cyber definition that concentrates on the use of technology, cyber as a risk is not for technology teams solely to remediate. It never has been. And yet it is our chief information officers (CIOs) and chief digital officers (CDOs), heads of technology, and IT managers who are counted on to secure budgets, manage audit findings exposing ineffective controls, and influence the strategic decisions of their c-level (executive) peers. Cyber spend that is tucked neatly into the technology budget is often endorsed as part of a broader technology business case. And yet the critical information assets that the cyber team protect, branch far wider than the remit of the CIO.

As part of our book research we asked CIOs what it means to them for the board to have an understanding of cyber. CIOs told us that an understanding and interest in cyber leads to more meaningful conversations, creates efficient outcomes, and facilitates important discussions on reputation.

We advocate for an appropriate level of technical literacy at a board level, along with the ability to evaluate cyber attacks and threats. For us, technical literacy and cyber literacy go hand in hand. Without a level of technical literacy, cyber literacy is almost impossible to fathom. *The Secure Board* is our passion project to uplift your knowledge and literacy. Directors need to be armed with enough information to feel confident that they can apply their knowledge to achieve their fiduciary responsibilities. Being educated regarding cyber means better understanding the context of the cyber board papers, being able to think ahead to consider possible future consequences (a key requirement of directors), being able to make an informed decision regarding a potential cyber investment, and knowing when to put your money in and when to take it out of a project. Directors act as a group in terms of the skill requirements of the board. All directors must assume responsibility for cyber, and not rely on a few cyber-savvy directors to ask all the questions and endorse all the 'asks' coming from the chief information security officer (CISO), much the same as a regulator would never rely on a handful of board members to consider the accuracy of quarterly financials.

The board's role when it comes to cyber is no different to their role in managing any other risk. They must monitor the performance and compliance and ensure the organisation is solvent. The functions of the board in setting the long-term strategy, resource allocation, and risk appetite are all key to the successful management of any enterprise risk. Cyber must be managed within the context of a reasonable risk appetite. This appetite, often set by boards, must be endorsed by directors who are well informed of threats and the risk context within which the organisation operates. Cyber is no different, and is central to both the prosperity and resilience of the organisation.

Many board members we spoke to in the lead-up to writing this book felt ill-equipped to deal with cyber, because they don't believe it remotely relates to traditional areas of director expertise and business acumen. Let us assure you that in our experience, 70% of governing cyber security risk as a board member is the same as managing any other business risk. The way that you assess risk, the metrics that you look for, and the questions that you ask are transferable. As our objective is to provide a sense of comfort around this topic, this is a time to pause, consider, and gain self-assurance that **70% of this you already know and do**. In our experience, 70% of cyber risk management can be achieved through good governance, traditional risk management practices (or staying current with the changing risk landscape relevant to your organisation), and decision-making principles that serve the best interests of your stakeholders. This book will educate you with the **elements that make up the other 30% of cyber risk management**, including a good understanding of your role in cyber, and establish a new level of confidence in this important area.

Across the world, 'boardrooms are better educating themselves on cyber risk and how to manage it at the enterprise level.

Governments are investing in cyber research, increasing guidance on cyber practices and technical issues, and facilitating information exchange between industry and government.'[7] The tide is slowly turning, and there is more to do to appreciate the abundance of information available in relation to cyber.

How to gain confidence that your organisation is cyber safe

'The board needs to trust that senior management has a long-term view of cybersecurity, with a strategic road map and plans in place to adequately protect information assets and IT systems, regardless of where and how new threats emerge.'[8]

It became apparent very quickly in our research for this book that directors look to the cyber strategy to gain confidence that their organisation is cyber safe, or is at least on a path to risk reduction. The presence of a cyber strategy and the seeking of board endorsement is certainly a lead indicator that the organisation has a focus on uplifting the security controls and meeting their legal obligations. **What we are keen for you to observe are the other corners of your organisation, where cyber risk may be hiding in plain sight.** Ernst & Young reports that two-thirds of businesses consider cyber security merely as an afterthought, instead of including it in the planning stages of new business initiatives.[9] Statistics such as these must be flipped on their heads. Recognising the impact of your company culture, enterprise-wide spend, key commercial partners, and your overall business strategy on cyber will paint a much clearer picture of the value of the CISO and their team in supporting the business performance.

If you haven't met your CISO (or equivalent), now is a great time to discover who is managing cyber risk, day to day. They also have a role to understand you, your peers on the board, and the role you play in achieving a cyber-safe organisation. The trust and commitment to each other's priorities is vital to managing risk for your organisation.

One of the key ways to uplift your knowledge is to recognise that there is always more to learn. All of us can benefit from advice, be it from a third-party advisor or the organisation's CISO (more on that in element 5). Having a baseline of cyber knowledge allows you to ask the right questions and understand the answers. It allows you to better manage risk for your organisation, fulfil your duties as a director, and lead your organisation through an ever changing economic world. There are parts of this book that may seem operational in nature to you. We are quite deliberate in sharing this with you to assist you to better understand the mechanics and depth of the information that sit behind board papers you receive and 'the ask' or decisions that come to you from your c-suite. Bear with us. Read on. We will always bring you, the reader, to a point of understanding the relevance and context of our words on the bigger board picture.

We have written this book after leading technology and security teams for decades, hearing of boards and committees signing off on strategies they couldn't understand, and endorsing recommendations for high-risk behaviour, the potential consequences of which they were blind to. As authors, our objective in sharing this knowledge is to inspire you to start the cyber conversation with the confidence gleaned from the pages in this book. We encourage you to take on a beginner's mind as you soak in the content. It can be read cover to cover or as a reference. As your board meeting agenda presents you with new cyber challenges, refer back to sections, summaries, and the key questions to ask of your CISO.

In 2020, the World Economic Forum assessed the impact and likelihood of global risks, with cyberattacks only outshone by climate change and natural disasters as more likely and with greater impact.[10] Closer to home, Darren Kane, Chief Security Officer at nbn, reminds us that 'the digitisation of the global economy means few businesses can expect to remain immune to a cyber breach and must prepare for the inevitable'.[11] Cyber is not a project or a program; it's a way of doing business. Regular investment, both financially in appropriate controls that consider technology, process, data, and people, for which we have coined the phrase *the security collective*, and through our personal learning agendas, is key to addressing and minimising the potential impact of this often intangible but very real risk.

A note about language throughout this book

As with most industries, there are terms in the security industry that are used interchangeably, and not necessarily appropriately. While we don't support one over another, for ease of writing and readability, we have chosen to use certain terminology consistently through the book.

Board: Within this book, references to a board, or boards, can be considered to incorporate sub-committees and boards of any nature, including corporations, government, not-for-profits, charities, family businesses, community boards, etc.

Chief Information Security Officer (CISO): Throughout this book, we use the term chief information security officer (CISO) as a blanket expression for security leadership. If your organisation does not have a CISO, it may be that management have assigned security-related activities to others, which is fine, as long as someone owns security, and that the messages you receive as a board are unfiltered, transparent, and fact-based when it comes to cyber risk. Other titles you may see include cyber security lead, head of information security, chief security officer, director of information security, and VP of information security.

Critical information assets: Our use of this term encompasses the literal sense of the words: information assets that are critical to the operation of an organisation and therefore must be protected. You may have heard these referred to as business information assets or even 'the crown jewels'. The identification of those assets deemed critical is key to understanding where to invest your security and compliance resources. These assets are owned by 'the business'.

Cyber: While some agree that the term 'information security' better describes the holistic nature of what this industry aims to achieve, the word cyber has grown in popularity since the 1990s as the coverall term for the secure use of information and communication technologies. As such, throughout the book, we use the term 'cyber' to refer to cyber security, information security, cyber safety, and security in general, but excluding physical security.

Director: We use the term 'director' to encompass all those who have fiduciary duties, including non-executive directors (NED), de facto directors, shadow directors, and nominee directors.

Incident/breach/event: We use 'incident' throughout the book to explain any case when unauthorised access (an individual or organisation with unapproved access) causes impact to the integrity, confidentiality, or availability of a system or systems. This could mean a breach of a network; a loss, theft, or destruction of data; exposure of passwords and usernames; or theft of intellectual property. A data breach is a type of cyber incident. When an incident occurs, it doesn't always mean information is compromised or breached, and at times can be purely the denial of a service (such as when an ecommerce site is deemed out of order) or the defacement of a website by a malicious third party. It also doesn't always mean a business interruption occurs when data is accessed or exfiltrated (when data is removed in secret), which can be the cause of incidents going unnoticed.

Information: In the sense that we use this term throughout the book, information refers to data, documents (hard and soft copy), and knowledge in any form that relates to the commercial nature of a business (such as intellectual property on paper, electronic, spoken, or recorded).

'The business': While it should be noted that IT and cyber are just as much a part of the business as marketing or the investments team, throughout the book we often use the term 'the business' to denote any department, stakeholder, or decision maker that is part of the wider organisation. This is done both through habit and because this may well be the language used by your head of technology or CISO.

The Security Collective: When we refer to 'the security collective', we are bringing together the pillars on which effective and robust cyber security is built on: people, process, data and technology. These pillars should be considered enterprise-wide, including operations, projects, audits, and business growth, as the collective group of factors required to secure your organisation.

ELEMENT 1

CYBER IS A BUSINESS RISK, NOT AN IT PROBLEM

'Trust is the currency of the 21st Century: The collaborative economy has turned trust into a commercial currency and triggered a new way of doing business driven by the reputation not only of brands but also consumers.'[12]

Rachel Botsman

A cyber attack on a business has universal implications. Every person working in and with the business contributes to protecting the company from a cyber incident. Incidents such as ransomware attacks are estimated to have cost US businesses more than $7.5 billion in 2019. During the pandemic of 2020, reports suggest that ransomware attacks grew a further 72%.[13] When you hear of a cyber incident, you never solely hear of how the technology was destroyed, or that, simply, systems were 'down'. The impact of an attack or incident on a business is, and must be, considered a serious threat of financial loss, business disruption, exposure of critical business information, and compromise to the reputation and brand, including consumer, employer, and supply chain. The impact of an attack can take down a whole organisation. And yet, when it comes to implementing controls and taking action towards cyber risk, the finger is often pointed at IT teams and CIOs, despite cyber being a business risk, not an IT problem.

It's a common theme throughout this book that the first step in addressing cyber risk is to understand it. As a director, you can and must educate yourself on cyber. This enables conversations at the board level about cyber risk and begins to normalise having a cyber risk conversation outside of the CIO's board paper. **If we only look at cyber as an IT problem, then our peer directors, stakeholders, and employee community will continue to believe it only warrants an IT response.**

'Cyber security researchers have identified a total of at least 57 different ways in which cyber-attacks can have a negative impact on individuals, businesses and even nations, ranging from threats to life, causing depression, regulatory fines or disrupting daily activities.'[14]

As a board member you play an important role in establishing and asserting the accountability of cyber risk through a broad understanding of the business functions surrounding cyber, the questions you ask, and to whom those questions are directed. The CEO's role is to provide clarity to the board, regulators, and employees on accountabilities and connect the dots on how these important functions work together to keep the business safe and be prepared in the event of an incident. The list below, which is by no means exhaustive, discusses those functions that sit outside the cyber remit and, in some cases, outside IT altogether, but play a role in the prevention, detection, and management of cyber security:

- Privacy – Privacy comprises the regulation, policies, and processes used to govern the collection and handling of personal data, such as credit information and medical and government records. The privacy officer is often a lawyer within your business, and all correspondence with the Privacy Commissioner or the Office of the Information Commissioner is handled by the privacy officer and legal team.

- Financial Crime – Financial crime is a relatively new business function to prepare for and manage economically motivated crime, including fraud, electronic crime, money laundering, terrorist financing, bribery and corruption, and insider dealing. These crimes take place with or without technology. Certainly, technology these days is often used as the channel through which these crimes are carried out. However, financial crime can be just as easily carried out in person, digitally, or as paper based.
- Data Governance – The governance of data includes the classification of business data and information by criticality. It is the processes, policies, and governance put in place to manage the use and quality of business data and information. Data governance must have a strategy that fits your organisation's maturity, and progresses as you do.
- Crisis Management – Crisis management and planning prepare for the business impact due to a natural or man-made disaster, and takes in facilities, customers, staff, and, most importantly, safety. Crisis management and planning should never be solely managed by IT.
- Business Continuity Plan (BCP) – BCP is the planning and management needed to return to essential business services following an unplanned event. Like crisis management, BCP includes facilities management and customer and staff safety, and is focussed on resilience and restoration.
- Disaster Recovery (DR) – DR is the planning and management needed to return to normal business operations following an IT failure. While DR may be needed as part of addressing a cyber attack, more often than not it is invoked due to an operational IT failure.

The above business functions all play a role in the protection, prevention, and response to a cyber attack. The board must have a level of comfort that these functions are working together with the aligned strategies and plans needed in the face of an incident.

Many incidents are as a result of employees reacting to an attack – usually via email, voicemail, or SMS – which allows a hacker access to your systems. As your employees have approved system access, along with a high level of trust, this access opens the doors for an adversary, making them appear legitimate to your systems and monitoring. Forrester's 2018 research estimates that 80% of data breaches have a connection to 'compromised privileged credentials', such as usernames and passwords.[15] With one quarter of compromised data traced back to insider incidents,[16] the criticality of employee education and awareness in cyber security is clear. The timely management of modifying or revoking system access when an employee changes roles or leaves the organisation is a critical step in cyber security protections. For peace of mind, and for the organisation to identify gaps to remediate, assessing maturity and compliance in the area of employee system access is a valuable audit activity.

As part of our research, CIOs and CISOs shared that, from time to time, the board, including the CEO, have not understood when something – for example, an incident or audit finding – isn't due to cyber; rather, it is an organisational risk (people, rather than systems).

We can learn from organisations that have had their data accessed by a malicious third party through an employee reacting to a phishing attack to further demonstrate why everyone within the business plays a critical role in avoiding attacks:

Sydney hedge fund Levitas Capital suffered a cyber incident in September 2020 when one of the founders opened a fake invitation to a Zoom meeting. The hacker created $8.7M worth of fake invoices. Fortunately, only $800,000 was lost through the attack, and the remaining funds to pay the fake invoices were stopped before the money cleared. According to government figures, this attack was one of almost 2,000 of its type in only five months. The fund was forced to close when their biggest client withdrew its funds, following the incident.

Australian National University's 2018 attack led to confidential information about student administration, financial management, and human resources being stolen. Access to the sensitive information was gained in early 2018 through phishing emails attempting to gain login credentials (username and password) of an employee. The sophistication of the phishing attack meant that the employee only had to open and view the email, as opposed to more common phishing attacks where a link needs to be clicked or an attachment opened.

In 2017 a ransomware called 'WannaCry' was delivered worldwide via email. It encouraged the email recipient to open an attachment which then released malware (a virus). Malware disrupts, damages, or gains unauthorised access to systems and information. WannaCry infected 250,000 machines in more than 150 countries. As a result, the National Health Service (NHS) in the UK had to cancel thousands of appointments and operations, and employees had to revert to using pen and paper, as the attack had impacted key business systems.

What often follows incidents such as these is a desire for the business to never find themselves in the same position again. Ever. However, this goal of prevention isn't always achieved, unless businesses change their collective mindset. What we also know is that an all-of-company approach to cyber security can and does make a difference to the board's understanding. In the pages that follow, we explore cyber across the enterprise, the role that culture plays in keeping organisations cyber safe, and the impact to customer trust if organisations don't have a 'joined up' cyber narrative.

Cyber and the enterprise

In 2019 it was expected that companies would spend more than $2 trillion on digital transformation, with 70% of organisations having a digital transformation strategy in place or building one.[17] With most businesses digitally enabled today, protecting company information and assets is essential for business growth and productivity, to prioritise customer experience and the company brand, attract and retain talented employees, and foster an effective relationship with regulators. While the development of the business strategy is an opportunity for the board, CEO, and management to demonstrate consideration, prioritisation, and commitment to these important areas, the business strategy also informs the cyber security strategy, associated investment, and the cyber risk appetite. (See element 2 for more information on setting risk appetite.)

One of the critical influencers of cyber security having a strategic presence is the CEO. The CEO is instrumental in understanding and advocating for cyber security awareness and shared accountability across the organisation and fostering a cyber security culture. Consumers are signalling a lower tolerance for cyber incidents involving their data, with 40% blaming the CEO personally for lapses in cyber security. Gartner predicts that by 2024, 75% of CEOs will be held personally accountable for cyber incidents that lead to injury or other physical damage.[18]

Cyber security must be at the top of the CEO agenda, not only in terms of a level of understanding of threats and controls but, most importantly, for reinforcing a cyber-aware culture through symbols. Best described by Jim Schleckser, CEO of the Inc. CEO Project, 'Symbols are extremely powerful in that they help enable people to do things and attribute meaning to their actions even when you as the CEO aren't in the room, so you need to manage them'.[19]

Cyber threats are the fourth concern to a CEO for growth prospects in 2020.[20] The CEO 'sets the bar' and models the desired culture with a cyber-risk focus across the enterprise, with employees understanding the threats and implications. We encourage the CEO to work with a change-management practitioner to carefully consider a plan for the CEO to demonstrate a personal and company commitment to cyber security through symbols and stories. Boards may choose to demonstrate engagement and support in similar ways. A good example is a board member attending industry events and sharing any cyber-related collateral with the CEO, CIO, and CISO, and encouraging discussion of the knowledge gained through these forums.

An important symbol by the CEO is the determination of the reporting line of the CISO and how many levels the role sits below the CEO in the organisational structure. The most common reporting line for the CISO is into the CIO, with the CIO reporting to the CEO. The CISO reporting to the Chief Risk Officer or Chief Legal Counsel are alternatives. Our research with CIOs and CISOs tells us that as long as the CISO message is not filtered to the board, it shouldn't matter who the role reports to. Reporting to the CIO (or chief technology officer) reflects the inter-connectivity with IT. Reporting into risk or legal provides independence, which could assist with risk-mitigation decisions not being overshadowed by IT constraints. Either way, we recommend that the CISO reports into a chief that sits on the executive leadership team. We do know of organisations where the CISO reports directly to the CEO, and we expect to see this trend continue.

The relationship between the CISO and the CEO is of on-going importance. The role this relationship plays is one of trust, and is key to the united front that the board should expect to see, regarding cyber. Not only is the CEO in a position of responsibility in relation to cyber security strategically but they are also responsible for the organisational culture being one that recognises and promotes a cyber-safe business environment.

The significance of a company culture of security

'Since cyber is everywhere, cyber awareness needs to be embedded everywhere. That means that cyber must be part of everyone's job in a very literal sense.'[21]

Culture is how people behave when no one is looking. And culture doesn't just happen. Culture involves everyone being accountable for calling out poor behaviour, speaking up, and being mindful of their own behaviour. Employees and stakeholders learn appropriate behaviour by looking up, so to speak. They receive direction, even subconsciously, as to what is considered right and acceptable behaviour. The culture of the organisation not only sets the behavioural norm. It plays a critical role in achieving your strategic objectives across the enterprise. If we have a cultural approach from the board that supports taking risks to achieve financial gain, but puts the organisation at greater cyber risk, this approach will filter down through the organisation via the CEO and management as an appropriate way of doing business. The role of the board in setting the overall company culture is no different from setting a culture of cyber security from the top down.

You would never hear someone suggest that workplace safety is only the concern of engineers who work on factory floors. We know, through years of injuries, deaths, and changes in the law, that in order to protect our employees, our reputation, and our bottom line, safety must be an enterprise-wide commitment. Despite the cliché that safety and cyber go hand in hand, the similar cultural focus required to embed them really can't be denied. Even the Australian privacy laws regarding mandatory reporting use the physical safety of the data owner as a test as to whether or not the commissioner should be alerted to a cyber incident that has exposed sensitive data.[22] Just like safety, the board, CEO, and senior executive walking the walk sets the expectations for the broader business. The risk of the opposite, a bottom-up culture, is that the security team are constantly pushing for employee engagement without senior role models demonstrating behaviours and symbols for employees to see. And, just like safety, a lack of a security-focussed culture has been seen to lead to very real incidents.

In 2017, American credit reporting agency Equifax experienced a cyber attack to the tune of 143 million sensitive data records. Upon analysis, they believe that their corporate culture was partly to blame. Post-incident, they set about addressing this as a preventative security measure. At the time of writing, Equifax are making it their business to share this revelation with the press, at conferences, and through corporate studies in order to focus the attention of all corporates on the importance of culture in the fight against cyber crime. Interestingly, the credit reporting agency was not heavily regulated at the time of the incident. Regulation can often lead to boards and CISOs being much more heavily focussed on compliance. It has been proven time and time again that a culture of compliance does not protect organisations. Even so, Equifax did not see the need to be diligent about protecting their critical information assets, because they were not going to be held accountable for it. While these credit reporting agencies were not held to high cyber security compliance standards like banks are required to by their regulator, they certainly hold the very same data that make banks a target of cyber attack. It is believed this organisation-wide culture of complacency led to a gap between IT policy development and execution. Furthermore, their business strategy was one of aggressive growth; however, their 'complexity and antiquated ... IT systems made IT security especially challenging. Equifax recognized the inherent security risks of operating legacy IT systems because Equifax had begun a legacy infrastructure modernisation effort. This effort, however, came too late to prevent the breach.'[23]

Mary Jo Hatch views culture as manifesting in three ways, which, when pared back, leaves you with beliefs, values, and visible, tangible artefacts.[24] This three-layered culture has been spoken of throughout a number of information security culture research papers as the basis of a cultural framework. But, interestingly, there has been an additional fourth layer: knowledge. The influence of knowledge on assumptions, values, and behaviours cannot be underestimated. This fourth layer, knowledge, has been added because cyber security knowledge cannot be assumed to be present.[25] Without this knowledge about cyber, including understanding threats, prevention, and resilience when it comes to cyber security, it is incredibly difficult for our employee communities to embody a culture of security. With this knowledge, organisations can make decisions not just about their cyber security risk approach but also apply this knowledge to put a cyber-risk lens over all commercial decisions.

How you create, foster, embody, and leverage a culture of cyber security depends on a number of factors unique to your organisation. Where boards must focus on security as part of a merger or acquisition, the head of marketing must understand the impact of partnering with a supplier that does not share your security values when it comes to protecting data. Where boards must focus on solvency, or lack thereof, your head of finance must understand the investment needed to protect the organisation's critical information assets to prevent long-term financial implications. Your head of human resources must understand that workforce planning may require investment in security leaders in the same way that you invest in sales leaders – both resources can be the difference between customer acquisition and retention. And while boards must understand cyber in terms of culture, strategy, finance, and risk, the CEO and their leadership team must understand these same factors, but in relation to enterprise-wide operations. When fulfilling one of your most important roles as a board – hiring the CEO – you have the opportunity to select someone who can bring values and behaviours aligned with the culture you want in the business. If you're seeking to drive a culture of security, this can only be achieved through honest board conversations about the culture you want to create. Talking about cyber can be uncomfortable and awkward as the board feels its way. Bringing in advisors and cyber experts to uplift the board's knowledge, and measure the culture when it comes to cyber, provides data points to which improvements can be planned.

If we return to the age-old analogy of safety, what was once unthought of, like seatbelts, safety switches, hard hats, and steel-cap boots, necessitates companies having had to adjust, because lives depended on it and regulators demanded it. At the time of writing this, regulators are beginning to use their powers to mandate that boards take responsibility for cyber. This mandate must translate into **a board-empowered CEO who**

can balance the requirements of the CISO and the regulator with the commercial operations and strategic delivery of the organisation's goals, which are, more often than not, focussed on serving and increasing their customer base.

Protecting customer trust

Australians are inherently trusting. We give our word with a handshake and often agree to transact with others on the basis of our own feelings of trust, or trust borrowed from a referring friend. What we have come to learn, with most organisations now offering digital services to consumers (B2C) and/or businesses (B2B), is that customers have an assumed level of trust that their data (and, sometimes, their money) is being cared for by a business as if it were its own. And inversely, companies have a level of trust that consumers have the capability and commitment to play their part in protecting their sensitive information. Notwithstanding commercial contracts and regulations, a breach of this trust in the event of an incident will lead to reputational damage, often resulting in loss of revenue. In 2020, the average cost of a data breach globally was $3.86M.[26] On average, reputational damage and business downtime accounted for 40% of total losses.[27] This reputational damage is clear when customers vote with their feet. In a 2019 global study, when broken out from our international peers, Australian responses suggested the percentage of customers who would hesitate to do business with an entity who had experienced a cyber incident, and those who would never return, was 43% for both decisions.[28] These figures show potential revenue loss that many businesses may never recover from.

The consequences of reputational damage – the goodwill on the balance sheet which is at risk – must be discussed, challenged, and agreed when risk appetite statements relating to cyber security are defined and approved. How an organisation engages with customers, and responds publicly in the event of an incident, will be imperative in retaining customer trust and loyalty. In element 2 we explore the enterprise-wide work required to prepare for an incident and the lessons you can gain from a 'safe learning environment' about how best to manage the impacts to customer trust. The board and third-party vendors should be included in these simulations. In our experience, it is clear accountabilities and stakeholder engagement that are often an oversight during the stress and chaos of an incident. An effective way to establish and encourage shared accountability and understanding is for another executive to have ownership of the reputation or brand risk. As a board, you should expect reputational risk to be part of the cyber security and chief risk officer updates to the board. As always, no matter who brings this topic to the boardroom table, protection and consideration for customer trust during a security incident is critical.

Most organisations that are transparent, honest, and forthcoming with information during a cyber incident are those that bounce back and retain the trust of their customers and the respect of their peers and regulators. Certainly, a great example of this is The Australian Red Cross Blood Service, during their incident of 2017. The incident occurred when a file containing information relating to approximately 550,000 prospective blood donors was publicly exposed. The incident, the result of human error of a third-party supplier, caused the Australian Red Cross Blood Service to notify affected individuals and the Office of the Australian Information Commissioner. After his investigation, the commissioner in a public statement praised the blood bank, stating that 'Australians can be assured by how the Red Cross Blood Service responded to this event. They have been honest with the public, upfront with my office, and have taken full responsibility at every step of this process', showing a commitment to securing personal information.[29]

Conversely, with customers able to feed back to organisations via social media when the expectations of their trust have not been met, Canva's cyber incident in 2019 demonstrates the power of the social platform. Canva's original communication to its community was labelled 'marketing fluff', as the online graphics giant served up their customer base with an email that led with positive news of their new t-shirt printing capabilities in the US before informing of the 'data breach' they had experienced.[30] With this feedback, Canva released an updated version of the email to their customers that communicated the heart of the matter. Businesses who 'fluff' the seriousness of a cyber incident can do further damage in the wake of an incident. On the topic of communications, announcements regarding incidents should be communicated formally by the CEO. While there are number of 'company lines' that can be pre-planned and practiced in these situations, in a time of crisis, being clear with your audience with details of what has occurred, what it's safe for you to disclose at the time (even if you can't give all the details), and when the next update will come will begin to rebuild, hold firm, or even increase your community's trust. Some organisations keep a running update of their cyber response activities via a website, such as Toll does, to keep their community up to date. See an example of Toll's updates here: https://www.tollgroup.com/toll-it-systems-updates.

Key lessons and reflections

While cyber attacks may infiltrate an organisation through electronic means, their cause and ultimate impact often lie far beyond their technical origins. As described above, there are financial, privacy, regulatory, governance, operational, and reputational impacts from cyber attacks that are managed by a broad range of stakeholders, with the CIO and the CISO being just two. While we always advocate for a united front coming to the board in the post-incident days to report, behind the scenes the CIO and CISO may not be the decision makers in the wake of all cyber incidents. No board likes to see finger pointing or executive in-fighting. While the technical root cause of a cyber attack is important to establish, of equal concern is a head of marketing, for example, who allows critical information assets to pass into the hands of a partner who fails to protect it. This, too, requires investigation to ensure that the right process and due diligence opportunities are afforded by the organisation's governance frameworks.

Managing cyber isn't obvious to most people outside of the security team. Business leaders need to be educated and confined to processes that can sometimes seem restrictive in order to play their part in the reduction of cyber risk. If the culture of 'Cyber is not an IT problem; it's a business risk' can be demonstrated through symbolic gestures and sign posts for staff, eventually the protection of critical information assets will become as second nature as donning a hard hat.

Areas for reflection

- When did the board last receive cyber training? How was it delivered, and by whom?
- How has reputational risk been considered in risk appetite, strategy, and/or reporting?
- Is cyber mentioned in the CEO's board updates, including progress relating to education and awareness for employees?
- Is cyber discussed at company briefings, investor briefings, or referenced when making business decisions?
- Has cyber been represented in the business strategy and annual report?
- How is the board, or audit and risk committee, proactively focussed on emerging risks?
- What symbols can we use to demonstrate our desire for a continuing cyber culture?

Questions to ask during a board meeting

- Where is all our data kept?
- Which organisations have access to our data? How is this managed and governed?
- Outside of the CIO, do other executives have the autonomy and authority to share sensitive information with third parties? (Please refer to 'The Business' Contributing To Cyber Risk on page 36 for context.)

- How often does the CEO meet with the CISO, one on one?
- Is the CEO working with the CISO to understand the importance of cyber across the enterprise?
- Has reputational risk been considered in this update, recommendation, or decision?
- What message will this send our customers about trust?
- How are our post-incident communications working to protect customer trust?
- Does executive remuneration include accountability for company-wide risk?

ELEMENT 2

TAKING A RISK-BASED APPROACH TO GOVERNING CYBER SECURITY

'Being the subject of a cyber-attack incident is not a crime – but how you respond to it in the future could be. Being prepared to respond to an incident, at a business level, not just with the technology, is absolutely critical.'

Gordon Archibald, partner, Cyber Security Services, KPMG

Cyber security is a broad and emerging topic, often with board updates provided in technical terms and presented by those deemed to be 'techos'. The pace at which cyber risk is shifting can be daunting, and it is instinctive to look to regulators to define in layman's terms what component of *the security collective* will 'keep you safe'. However, regulatory standards alone will not protect any business, as no one can move at the pace of these threats. Threats will materialise and exploit vulnerabilities in any business. A phishing attack is a good example of an incident occurring which is not a control failure but a human error – nothing will protect the business from a phishing email that an employee opens or clicks on a contained link which allows the perpetrator access to the business systems. Organisations can no longer have a zero tolerance for cyber attacks, as most large-scale incidents are out of our immediate technical control. All stakeholders must understand that it is not prevention but detection, resilience, and response to attacks that will see a business bounce back effectively and efficiently, post-incident.

This is the primary reason for writing this book: not to instil fear, but to talk through all aspects of cyber security, what to look for in your board papers, what to ask your leaders, and to provide reassurance that you can grasp this persistently changing business risk.

Indeed, 70% of governing cyber security risk as a board member is truly the same as managing any other business risk. The way that you assess risk, the metrics that you look for, and the questions that you ask are transferable. Again, as our objective is to provide a sense of comfort around this topic, this is a time to pause, consider, and gain self-assurance that **70% of this you already know and do**.

This element discusses how to govern cyber risk the way you do any other business risk, plus how to oversee the 30% that is complex and technical. Examples of what makes up the 30% includes cyber risk management, incident response, risk mitigation plans, and controls which are technical in nature.

The importance of risk appetite statements

Companies that manage cyber security risk effectively define and analyse their exposure. More than a third (34%) of ASX 100 companies surveyed have clearly defined their cyber security risk appetite. However, 38% of companies have yet to define their risk appetite, which could have implications for how management makes decisions around cyber security risk controls.[31]

Risk appetite statements are a simple yet effective component of risk management. Definition of the risk appetite for information and cyber security should be facilitated by someone with subject matter expertise and the ability to understand and articulate the consequences for the entire business. Business participants in the definition of the risk appetite may include other IT senior leaders (including the CISO), line 1 and 2 risk managers, and the executives (or delegates) for customer, data, and compliance.

It is tempting for an organisation to have a conservative appetite for cyber risk, and it usually requires significant investment and monopolises the annual project portfolio for several years. This highlights the importance of establishing a risk appetite that is realistic for your business. The defined risk appetite informs the initiatives and roadmap to implement the cyber security strategy, how decisions are made, and other business activities. These initiatives and tasks must be assessed for effectiveness – how do they minimise risk? – and not only the return on investment. The discussion between the board and management on how the risk appetite was collectively defined by management and associated tolerances is valuable. This is an opportunity for management to demonstrate to the board the cross-company engagement and collaboration in defining the risk appetite for information and cyber security, and understanding the importance of working within appetite. As a board member you should expect this holistic view from management and understand consequences to comfortably approve the risk appetite. Through our research, 100% of CISOs and 72% of directors told us that the board relies on, values, and gains confidence from the cyber security function maintaining risk appetite.

When working on the assumption that risk appetite is considered in making business decisions, we contemplate what the following organisations would have learnt from these incidents.

Facebook: Facebook was charged after misleading customers about the extent to which the company's third parties could access and utilise their personal information. Although a US$100 million settlement was reached with the Securities and Exchange Commission, the company was then fined US$5 billion for deceiving users of the social media platform about access to sensitive information.

Equifax: It was found that signals relating to inadequate risk management capabilities at Equifax were ignored, with no evidence of regular cyber security audits, employee training, or incident response plans. It took Equifax two months to discover that there had been an incident which impacted 148 million people. As a result, the CEO stood down, another executive was charged with insider trading after selling shares before the cyber attack was disclosed to customers and media, and a new CISO was hired.

When discussing and deciding on risk appetites in relation to cyber security and reputation, we recommend 'testing' the proposed appetite rating against several scenarios on an on-going basis.

In the case of cyber risk treatment, it is risk mitigation, not elimination

'Even the most prepared of organizations can suffer a cybersecurity breach or data loss – and according to surveys, the majority of large organizations already have. The impact can be substantial – ranging from fines, lost revenue and out-of-pocket costs for credit monitoring to reputational damage, negative publicity, and operational slow-downs.' [32]

Board and management discussions relating to cyber security have shifted over the past decade from investment in risk elimination to a risk-based assessment of the cost of controls against the exposure. With the pace and sophistication of emerging threats, investment in technology alone is no longer a safeguard.

As with all business risks, management and the board need to manage and govern risk within an agreed risk appetite. Our thinking was further validated in our research when some CISOs told us that the number one thing that boards rely upon to gain confidence in the cyber risk position is the CISO reporting that they are 'maintaining the risk within appetite'. This statement plays an important role in the approach and cost of managing risk, as well as assessing the four main risk-treatment strategies. In the context of the treatment of cyber risk, here are some risk treatment examples:

Mitigate – develop a strategy inclusive of *the security collective* to minimise risk, with the intended outcome to bring the risk within appetite.

Avoid – if a new system or third-party relationship is being considered, and adequate assurance of data sovereignty or protection mechanisms cannot be demonstrated or requirements met, the vendor relationship should not progress, in order to avoid the risk.

Transfer – taking out a cyber security insurance policy, or establishing a relationship with a strategic partner to provide 24x7 cyber security monitoring, detection of possible attacks, and triage of unusual activities, can transfer some of the risk away from your organisation's responsibility.

Accept – implementing two-factor authentication (2FA) to provide customers with two different ways to verify their identity, and making the decision to use 2FA voluntary for the customer, is an example of the acceptance of an access-control risk.

These risk treatments are usually included in risk reports prepared for the board by the CRO, CIO, or CISO, and must be updated regularly to reflect any change to your organisational risk position.

No matter our approach to risk-appetite positions, risk-treatment plans, or the overall quantification of risk, the reality in this day and age is that security incidents will happen. Knowing how likely and how often you may be exposed to this form of risk is all part of knowing what risk treatment to select. Furthermore, understanding how quickly your organisation can *stem the flow* and hold off an adversary from perpetuating any further damage is the key to making effective risk-based decisions.

Resilience

'While compliance with good practice is important, the real cyber security challenges are to make business and technology choices that reduce exposure and minimise opportunity for attackers.'[33] – Aaron Steele

No organisation is 100% safe from vulnerability, threat, exploitation, or human error. The important thing is that you are resilient. Knowing your organisation is resilient can take time and, like everything else in this book, is born from trust that there are sufficient measures in place. A survey conducted across eight Asia-Pacific nations found that over a third (35%) of Australian respondents still don't feel their organisation is cyber resilient.[34] Part of grasping how resilient your organisation would be to a cyber attack is to understand the investments made in monitoring, defence, detection, and response. We cannot use compliance to frameworks or regulatory requirements to establish our resilience, as these are often assessed at a point in time. Should investment in maintaining controls not be available, our resilience to current threats can be impacted. Cyber security is like painting the Sydney Harbour Bridge. While there is no question that you must be thorough in everything you do, by the time you have finished painting, it's time to go back to the other end and start again. There is no guarantee that the actions we take today will stand the test of time in terms of being resilient to future attacks. Board papers are always historical. By the time you receive information, there is a chance it is out of date, based on the changing threat landscape and technology on which your business operates. It is important to regularly ask for updates as to cyber resilience measures and the effectiveness of these controls.

A valuable guide to your resilience to cyber attack can be brought together by your CISO (or equivalent) for your review. The story to be told will need to cover:

- Whether your critical processes can continue to operate during, and in the wake of, a cyber attack – do you have disaster recovery (defined in element 1), system redundancy, or fail-over that would allow your operations to continue, even if not at full capacity?
- How your current security strategy protects the critical information assets and addresses threats, old and new – legacy operating systems need to be protected as well as newer systems from emerging threats.
- Security capabilities – has the security operating model been established against the security strategy and business operations to ensure that both day to day and in the face of a crisis, the right services can be drawn on, internally and with trusted outsourced partners?
- How are decisions about security balanced with desired product innovation?
- Understanding the nature and severity of both internal and external security-related audit findings across the enterprise (not just for IT).
- Case studies of peer incidents comparing *How would we have fared?* in a similar scenario.
- Response plans – know that your organisation has a plan to respond to incidents efficiently that has been practiced. Resilience is about recovering quickly, as well as effectively. While practicing your response to cyber security events may not feel like a valuable use of the board's time, rehearsing your response and knowing everyone's role could save your organisation critical time in the face of a crisis.
- Do you have a culture that promotes doing the basics well?

Key lessons and reflections

Cyber resilience involves a matrix of activities – no single action or investment will guarantee a short down time, isolation of a threat, and minimal impact to operations. While the CISO and CIO can undertake both tactical and strategic actions to improve resilience, further risk can be reduced through board engagement in cyber, good governance, cyber-specific risk management, response practice, and recovery planning.

Areas for reflection

- When discussing and approving risk appetite statements, has management clearly articulated the pros and cons of the proposed rating? Which scenarios have been played out to test understanding?
- Do I feel comfortable and reassured that cyber risk is managed within appetite?
- Do I have the information I need to oversee cyber risk?

Questions to ask during a board meeting

- Do we feel confident that our risk-appetite statement is realistic as it pertains to cyber?
- What cyber threats do we face?
- What did we learn from our last internal audit relating to cyber? What actions or decisions have we made as a result?
- Have we quantified cyber risk and modelled the financial implications of a cyber attack?
- How are we protecting customer data?
- What are the significant risks the board are willing to take?
- What are the significant risks the board are not willing to take?
- Does the board need to establish clearer governance over risk appetite, tolerance, and oversight?

- What is the magnitude of the risks we are now exposed to?
- How long can this organisation survive, if we have to stop operating?

Question to ask during or post-cyber attack

- Can we continue to operate throughout the incident investigation?
- Have we triggered any business continuity or crisis-management plans to be invoked? (more on this in the section titled, *The Role of the Board...*, page 51)
- Have we undertaken or considered independent investigations to validate our findings?
- Have we breached any legal or regulatory obligations? (Many organisations will choose to speak with the regulator, even when thresholds are not met for disclosure/reporting.)
- Have we spoken with our key partners and stakeholders in relation to third-party impacts and contractual obligations?
- Could this incident happen again?

'THE BUSINESS' CONTRIBUTING TO CYBER RISK

'The last ten years of IT have been about changing the way people work. The next ten years of IT will be about transforming your business.'

Aaron Levie, CEO, Box

Contrary to popular belief (of business stakeholders), the security team and the CISO do not own business risks. They do not decide on which risks to address and which to accept. The CISO is tasked with defining and implementing the cyber security strategy and leading the organisation in protecting the business's data assets. In order to do this, the CISO relies on business stakeholders to understand and inform them on which data is most critical and/or sensitive. Many organisations find the business identification and classification (sensitivity) of data a significant undertaking. Often, we have experienced business stakeholders attempting to push this activity back to IT, or the cyber security team. Having the business understand their role as owners of risk, owners of data, and the role they play in protecting data is important. To reiterate, cyber is a business risk, not an IT problem, as outlined in Element 1.

Once the business understands the criticality of new and existing business information assets, the CISO is positioned to effectively establish a strategy to protect them. New business information assets can be introduced through projects, including strategic initiatives or new regulatory compliance requirements, and they must also be classified. Often, the CISO will refer to the protection of critical information assets as 'protecting the crown jewels'. It is best practice to discuss the classification of information assets, and to reference them in contracts, when putting vendor contracts in place, as you are trusting the third party with your critical data. If the third party experiences a cyber incident, it will have reputational and financial consequences for your organisation. Examples of sharing sensitive information with third parties include:

- Subscribing to a cloud-based service, like Salesforce, which requires the procurement team to engage with the CISO to understand if sensitive information will be stored 'in the cloud' and where that data will be stored (data sovereignty) to ensure that regulatory requirements and company policies are met
- Engaging with a third party to deliver business initiatives, by building either a mobile application or website, which requires the organisation to share or provide access to sensitive data
- Outsourcing part or all of a business function; for example, a contact centre which records customer calls, or the management of content for the company website. Both examples entail the provider gathering and overseeing the organisation's sensitive information

Unfortunately, at times, the decision to share critical data with a vendor is made by staff in isolation. While IT and procurement governance processes may be perceived as bureaucratic, they are in place to protect the reputation and revenue of the business. Often, employees have the delegation to purchase IT systems and services on a corporate credit card, avoiding critical governance processes. Not only can this result in sensitive business information being shared without a contract in place but it also provides an entry point for cyber hackers that IT is not aware of. This activity is often referred to as Shadow IT, which we cover later in this element.

We can learn from the 2018 cyber incident at PageUp, an online recruitment management platform. For many Australian organisations, subscriptions to PageUp had been established without going through procurement governance processes, or paid for on a company credit card. The incident also resulted in debates regarding the sensitivity of the information that had been exposed. Many PageUp subscribers took comfort that customer data was not lost. It was a critical example to broaden the perspective on sensitive data, as the incident exposed personal details of job applicants – home address, date of birth, salary – a breach which the job seeker associated with the prospective employer, not PageUp. This demonstrates the imperative for the criticality of business information assets to be assessed with a broad lens. A good question that we consider is: *If this were to appear on the front page of the paper tomorrow, would I make the same decision?*

As reported in Conscious Governance, 'One thing has become abundantly clear: cyber security is no longer an IT issue and is more than just a risk management priority. To meet the cyber security challenge will require an enterprise-wide approach to the identification, detection, response and recovery of cyber risk.'[35]

Procurement and third-party vendors

'Every single bit of information, every system, every network is a target [and] every link in the [supply] chain is a potential vulnerability.' [36] – Christopher Wray, director, FBI, October 2018

In 2017, the Australian Stock Exchange surveyed the boards of listed companies on the ASX100 about their approach to cyber security. In their response to questions regarding third parties, just 11% of Australian boards had a clear understanding of where their company's key information or data assets were shared with third parties.[37] When it comes to protecting critical information assets, one of the key risks to your business is beyond your walls and somewhat out of your sphere of control – and that is third party risk. While it is fast becoming a cliche, with some organisations engaging with literally hundreds of third parties, a security control failure is a case of when, not if. In 2020 the Ponemon Institute revealed that 53% of organisations have experienced 'one or more data breaches caused by a third party', costing an average of $7.5 million to remediate.[38] Engaging with third parties can require you and your organisation to respond to incidents that are beyond your walls and sphere of control. The sharing of data has become commonplace in this digital age. It supports organisations to prosper; increases customer retention; improves customer relationships, as you can serve them better the more you know about them; and it can also reduce costs for your business. These benefits, though, may not outweigh the cost and reputational damage of a third-party cyber incident.

We can learn from a number of high-profile third-party cyber incidents, both here and abroad, that these attacks can not only cause commercial risks but also safety risks to customers and members of the public. Whether known to your organisation or not, the risks that organisations accept by agreeing to partner with a third party can be significant:

- In July 2020, WA Health suspended its use of a third-party paging service after sensitive information communicated over the service was found on a public-facing website. The information shared included doctor-to-doctor discussions and child protection updates. The Department of Health in WA immediately requested the pager service be disabled. At the end of the day, this service is needed to conduct business, and therefore a risk-based discussion is required, should they continue with this third-party engagement, once the incident has been remediated.[39]

- In January 2020, it was reported that online retail giant Amazon fired several employees after they leaked private customer data to an undisclosed third party for the second time in six months.[40] Customers had to be notified that their email addresses and phone numbers had been leaked to a third party, which was in violation of their policies. The good news is that the responsible employees were fired, which provides a deterrent for others who consider doing the same thing. However, the public often only sees the headline of Amazon's brand doing the wrong thing in their third-party interactions.

When it comes to the business engaging third parties, the importance of taking a risk-based approach to governing third parties can be weighed up with the knowledge of the data assets the third parties would have access to. Again, it's not just about the systems that the third party uses to house the data; it's about their policies governing how they treat that data, transfer that data, purge that data, company culture, employment contracts referencing privacy, etc. Working with third parties has become a part of everyday business, but third parties can and will continue to cause cyber incidents and reputational damage. Third-party engagement is now recognised by regulators as a key risk for organisations. Prudential authorities, such as Australian Prudential Regulatory Authority (APRA), now require organisations to put assurance programs in place to establish all of the third parties which the business is involved with, what data they have access to, and assess the risk of any transactions performed with that data, based on the effectiveness of security controls.

Unfortunately, not all third parties will align with your security standards. This increases risk, as any data you share with them, or access you provide to your systems, is potentially immediately exposed by way of association. While third parties that don't align with your security values put your organisation at risk, those assessed as having appropriate controls cannot be left to their own devices. Any assessment or assurance can only give you confidence at that point in time. Governance programs, regular assessments, and open dialogue between your organisation and theirs is key to risk reduction and risk management. It is critical that your organisation is confident in the third-party access and use of your data.

Third-party assurance programs should endeavour to:

- Establish the effectiveness of security controls which a third party has in place
- Ensure your agreements cover protection measures, should cyber incidents occur, or should the security posture of either organisation change
- Have a process for the selection of strategic partners, providing due diligence as to cyber-risk practices and treatment of third-party data
- Assess third-party risk, not just for compliance sake but with a risk lens

Third party assurance isn't free. Whether your organisation soaks up the resource requirement internally or a third party is used, it can be a big endeavour to assess and keep up with the risk that third parties pose to your organisation. Use of global and industry standards to assess and implement security controls can assist in reducing this cost, as everyone is 'singing from the same hymn sheet', to an extent.

As a board, you can encourage a culture of being an organisation that takes security seriously in all your dealings – not difficult to deal with, but thorough in your approach to security risk.

As a side note, while they are not squarely in the definition of a third party, you should consider your subsidiaries as third parties if they are distant relatives to your parent company. Often, they are trusted to access your network and share your data, but their culture when it comes to risk may differ significantly from yours.

Shadow IT

In all organisations, processes, policies, and governance are in place to define and guide appropriate decisions. Shadow IT, or business-initiated IT, is when business stakeholders buy, build, or use IT systems outside of the processes and policies defined to govern IT decisions. Some organisations allow business units to put IT systems in place independently, providing they meet governance requirements.

Shadow IT usually occurs when business stakeholders do not understand the governance process, or they consider the governance bureaucratic. With IT systems now easier to consume than ever, thanks to the cloud, they can often be subscribed to on a credit card, without a corporate contract in place. This creates a risk that sensitive business information is being shared without any understanding of where that information is stored, how it is used, and without contractual recourse in the event of an incident. It also provides a new entry point for cyber hackers which IT will not be aware of, as it has not been through the relevant governance processes. **To put this in a broad context, the board has approved investment for the CISO to implement a strategy to improve cyber resilience while business colleagues are creating new risks, which is counterintuitive.**

To provide further context, this is a trend which is 'pervasive and accelerating'. Gartner recently found that applications housed outside of IT (part of what's referred to as Shadow IT) represent 30% to 40% of IT spending in large enterprises, and other research by Everett Group suggests that up to 50% is spent outside of IT.[41] Which executive will be held accountable in the event of an incident?

Projects

Organisations deliver change through projects. This change through projects to customers, partners, and employees can be to meet compliance requirements, strategic initiatives, and to keep business operations efficient and effective. Projects will deliver new processes, new people, new capability which can be met through upskilling, hiring or partnering, and new systems. These new processes, partners, and systems can potentially create new risks for the business. The cyber security team must have on-going engagement, from early on in the project lifecycle through to transitioning the project into 'business as usual'. The process to engage the cyber security team should be defined as part of the organisation's project methodology. Throughout the project lifecycle, the cyber security team will either lead or participate in assessments to ensure that the organisation continues to operate within the cyber-risk appetite. The areas that should be assessed throughout the project should include:

- New or existing information assets – strategic projects or compliance requirements may result in the business storing new information assets, or modify the way existing business assets are consumed and managed. The cyber team work with the project team and information business owners to assess the information assets against existing controls and identify any new exposures. It is good practice for the project to fund the remediation of any new exposures as a result of the project. Without this approach, the organisation has increased risk exposure, and the expectation will be for the cyber team to minimise the risk without appropriate funding, resourcing, or prioritisation.

- New IT solutions – implementing a new system to deliver on strategic initiatives or to meet a compliance requirement, the cyber team assess the information being stored in the systems or information flowing through the system, where the data is stored, both the primary and the backup, and contribute to the contract negotiation to ensure that information is gathered, stored, and protected to meet the business and regulatory expectations, as well as appropriate compensation in the event of an incident.

- Modifications to existing IT solutions – in the ever-changing IT landscape, partnering with other organisations is common. These relationships can be short term, to deliver a project, or a long-term arrangement which embarks on outsourcing.

Both scenarios require people outside of the organisation to access internal systems which store business information. This activity is the accountability of the business; for example, who has access and where they reside (for any offshore resources, this is vitally important). The cyber team assess the risk of these access changes, determine how system access will be monitored and managed, and review the vendor contract to ensure appropriate clauses are in place relating to how information is managed and protected.

- System access management – in the event of a new system being introduced, the business establishes what access is granted to this system and to whom. The cyber team then assess how access to the system will be managed – for new employees where the level of system access must be determined, modifications to system access if an employee changes roles, and how (quickly) system access is revoked when an employee leaves the business. The team also assess if this access management is automated or a manual solution. A manual approach is at risk of human error and must be reflected in the risk profile. You can expect this to be a finding as part of the annual IT controls audit.

The outcome of these assessments often results in a risk assessment being created for the project. The risk assessment will articulate the risk, exposure to the business, the controls in place, when the risk will be mitigated, and the person accountable. Prior to the project going live, it must be determined if the risk will be accepted or if the project will be delayed until the risk can be minimised or mitigated. As a board member, the person who makes the decision to accept the risk should be of interest to you. The person making the decision, usually an executive, may not understand the breadth of possible consequences by accepting the risk; for example, reputational risk.

Innovation

'It is no longer possible for companies to innovate first
and provide for security and privacy second.' [42]

With business disruption and growth aspirations on the strategic agenda, organisations are seeking to innovate to compete and increase market share. Balancing innovation with risk is key, so as to not stifle progress. The business must not fear security when innovating and creating products to serve their customers (current and future), but spend time to understand the true implications of not addressing security, and that embedding security doesn't always mean a roadblock on the road to market. Business stakeholders engaging with the cyber security team on a regular basis, and developing a productive working relationship between teams, will provide the platform to operate within appetite while innovating.

Security culture (often labelled education and awareness)

'In the latest Notifiable Data Breaches Statistics
Report from the Office of the Australian Information
Commissioner, human error accounted for one third
(34 percent) of data breaches, from April to June, that
allowed hackers access to information.' [43] Australian
Cyber Security Magazine, January 2020

It has long been suggested that people are the weakest link when it comes to cyber security. At times, this is in the shape of a negligent staff member or contractor who deliberately shares a password, or a malicious insider who uses their access (or steals someone else's) to privileged data for financial gain. These are all insider threats that have the potential to cause havoc across your organisation. And insider threats are most definitely on the rise. A 2020 Ponemon report found a 47% increase in insider-caused cyber security incidents at companies worldwide since 2018. Both the frequency and cost of insider threats have increased dramatically. The overall average cost is \$11.45 million this year, a 31% increase since 2018, according to the report.[44]

But incidents occur that are all too often caused by a lack of knowledge or misfortune. To address incidents caused by accidental employee behaviour, our auditors, regulators, strategic advisors, and vendors alike suggest that we must empower our employees with awareness and education regarding cyber security. There is an assumption that with the right information, people will act and behave appropriately. But raising awareness is really just a part of the solution. Alone, it cannot change attitudes or influence behaviour. This does not mean that organisations should steer away from cyber-awareness activities. But, **rather than informing, we need to spend more time helping staff to understand the role they play and fostering and demonstrating desired behaviours.** As you might imagine, this comes back to having a cultural environment that encourages asking questions about appropriate secure behaviours, has consequences for inappropriate or high-risk behaviours, and provides staff with avenues to gain more information relevant to their role.

If you are to review a security strategy that suggests that an awareness program is planned, this is a great start, because, in a 2019 survey, Australian organisations cited 'culture, education, and awareness' as the lowest investment priority to improve cybersecurity maturity.[45] Cyber security education leaders SANS Institute have raised the concern that we are investing millions in security technologies and yet we continue to wonder why our staff fall for phishing attacks and open the door to ransomware.[46] If your organisation is planning efforts to combat the human impact of cyber security, this should be considered as important as investing in any technical control. What we will say, though, is that you should question the objectives and how the awareness program will be measured in terms of influence for behaviour change, not simply gather statistics as to the reach of the message. Awareness is often one dimensional and one way. But influence to change behaviours comes from the tone from the top, aligned values, and trusted relationships.

A note about customer education regarding cyber security

While organisations certainly have a duty of care regarding cyber security when it comes to their customers, there is a line to be drawn. While data is in the care of a business, most would agree they have a moral and/or legal obligation to care for that data. Organisations can provide guiding principles to their customers regarding the security controls that are part of their transaction or trade. However, giving customers too much advice could adversely affect an organisation, should things go wrong. While advising or recommending strong passwords or the use of two-factor authentication is a sound starting point for security measures, there is so much about a consumer's environment and circumstances that organisations will never know about and cannot control. As such, it is wise to allow consumers to seek their own cyber security knowledge and protection measures for use in their day-to-day lives. Given that consumers will often act in a way that puts them at higher risk of cyber crime, this is often due to a lack of knowledge. This knowledge is readily available through sources in Australia, such as staysmartonline.gov.au, cyber.gov.au, and the Office of the eSafety Commissioner, https://www.esafety.gov.au.

As a business or as a service provider, your role is to protect the data that a customer entrusts to you to the best of your ability. If a consumer 'leaves the door open' to their data, *they* are accountable for any wrongdoing that occurs. While this may sound dismissive and cold-hearted, there is only so much an organisation can invest in security before handing over the baton to the end user to carry forward responsibility.

In the case of a cyber incident, the duty of care changes, of course. The organisation must work to restore safety and security to the impacted consumer and regain their trust, but also support those customers whose data was not impacted yet who may feel even more exposed and in the dark. It is a complex web of communications and support that is required post-incident.

In the end, organisations will often provide guidance by means of a book of tips, a webpage on their online store that provides guidance, or proactively reaching out to customers with suggested products and services to provide strong cyber security controls. No matter what level of support an organisation provides, it must be commensurate with the level of responsibility the organisations can take in the wake of a consumer-side cyber security incident.

Key lessons and reflections

In 2021, cyber is expected to be a $6 trillion business, more profitable than illicit drug trade.[47] Boards are in a great position to influence the approach of cyber security by actively challenging management to view their strategic activities through a cyber risk lens. Furthermore, directors and the CEO can encourage management to take a long-term view of security across the enterprise. Consistently considering and questioning the presence of security (possibly ad nauseum) will eventually bring it into the everyday behaviours – into the organisation's values, strategy, and language.

In our collective 45 years of experience, often we have seen cyber incidents occur when processes and policies have not been adhered to. As a board, you can assist with business adherence with these tips:

- Advocate that the business is accountable for understanding and classifying their business information assets; for example, customer details, credit card numbers, bank account details
- All IT-related purchases must go through the procurement governance process
- The Procurement Governance process needs to include an assessment by the cyber security team
- The credit card acceptable use policy must include not purchasing IT software and hardware (excluding consumables)

- The CEO sets the tone for business adherence and the consequences when not met
- Identity (knowing who someone is and their role) and access management (managing what they have access to) must be a priority, not an afterthought
- Third-party risks must be managed across not only procurement but through M&A conversations
- Subsidiaries must align, for the most part, with parent company security principles and policies; this is non-negotiable, if they are to share data
- Culture plays an enormous role in the attitudes towards the protection of data in an organisation

Areas for reflection

- Do I understand how I could inadvertently be contributing to risk? Does the board comply with security policies and practices of the organisation? (For example, do board members comply with password complexity policies?)
- Would I support the acquisition of an organisation that experienced a breach in the past?

Questions to ask during a board meeting

- Do we know who has access to our critical information assets? How is this monitored and managed?
- What happens in the event a key supplier is hacked?
- Are we only considering 'security awareness', or are we seeking secure behaviour?
- In our security team, how many people are focussed on security technologies, and how many are focussed on the behaviours of our people?
- How are projects across the business considering cyber security risks that they may create, or acknowledge the controls their innovation may require? For example, how has

security been considered in regard to a finance or HR team planning to outsource payroll to a third-party cloud-based payroll company based offshore?

- How often does the CEO meet with the CISO, one on one?
- Are we doing everything we can for our customers to protect their data that we hold?

THE ROLE OF THE BOARD BEFORE, DURING, AND AFTER A CYBER SECURITY INCIDENT

'I am convinced that there are only two types of companies: those that have been hacked and those that will be. And even they are converging into one category: companies that have been hacked and will be hacked again.'

Robert S. Mueller III, former Special Counsel for the United States Department of Justice

In the face of a crisis, no amount of planning will prepare an organisation for the eye of the storm, or the aftermath. No incident will run perfectly according to the incident response plan, or in line with your most recent simulation scenario. In real life, there will be absent decision makers. There will be third parties who are challenging to manage. There will be events that are considered cyber incidents that are later discovered to be false positives. And there will be errors in judgement by clients and customers which lead to weeks of investigations, only to find that they had been too quick to report a suspicious situation (which, we admit, is better than not reporting it at all). Essentially, it is relationships, collaboration, and as much planning as possible that will guide you through a cyber incident. In your time as a director, you may be fortunate enough to hear nothing of cyber attacks, other than the CISO's metrics showing thwarted attempts and the details you read of the misfortunes of others in the press. Whether you are involved in a large-scale incident or simply participate in an annual drill, the lessons and knowledge you can glean will be invaluable. The role of the board before, during, and after a cyber incident cannot be underestimated, especially in the current legal and regulatory climate.

Not all technology incidents are cyber incidents

Preparing for, responding to, resolving, and recovering from a cyber security incident involves multiple business areas. Cross-company collaboration provides cognitive diversity to avoid 'groupthink' and develop a productive team which is critical in the event of a crisis. In our research, a director shared that 'collaboration and communication will also provide comfort, because you know management is working together and considering all alternatives. Anyone working alone or in a limited bubble tends to cause more weakness. A team approach is always much stronger, mitigating risk.'

The accountabilities across businesses during incidents or events are often confused, as roles are unclear or have not been well defined. In the event of a cyber incident, it is imperative that the different event types are understood, and roles and responsibilities have already been clarified. Key business capabilities involved in preparedness and response to incidents are fairly standard across businesses, globally. These include:

Business Continuity Planning (BCP) – usually led by the chief operating officer or chief risk officer, with a unified group of representatives from all business units, they undertake a business impact analysis to define essential business services to inform a plan to return these services to operational, following a business interruption. The COO also has overall accountability for the development, documentation, and sponsorship of BCP-incident-simulation exercises for the organisation.

Crisis Management – acknowledging that crisis management activities often have the same executive accountable as business continuity planning, a crisis and a business interruption are, in fact, separate events which require independent thinking, planning, and responding. Crisis management is the organisation's preparedness and management of an emergency as a result of a natural or man-made disaster, events that are outside of our control. Examples of such a crisis or emergency include natural disasters (e.g., floods and fires), transportation accidents (including aviation), and pandemics. In a crisis management event, the accountable executive manages the activities in the immediate first hours and emergency response efforts.

Disaster Recovery (DR) – led by the chief information officer, disaster-recovery incidents and activities are technology-focussed. Disaster-recovery planning and simulation preparedness focusses on restoring applications and systems to resume normal business operations. A disaster recovery event may be caused by a power outage to an office building or data centre, or a failure in IT hardware.

If the scale of an incident is large enough, what is initially perceived to be an isolated cyber incident that is managed through IT triage and management can escalate to invoke crisis management. Engaging with a third party to facilitate annual incident response simulations, which include both cyber with BCP, DR, and/or crisis management, is extremely valuable to assess preparedness and highlight areas for improvement.

In the unfortunate situation of any of these three events, communication is paramount. Communication requirements may vary by event type. Accountabilities should be agreed as part of planning activities and remain consistent across these types of events to avoid confusion:

- regulatory notification and reporting – chief risk officer or general counsel

- informing and updating the board – chief executive officer
- customer communication – chief executive officer or chief customer officer
- employee briefings and communication updates – chief people officer
- media briefings – chief executive officer, chief marketing officer, or public relations representative
- relevant IT vendors – chief information officer or chief information security officer

Response

In the midst of a crisis, the board may feel they are a fifth wheel. It may be believed by directors that log monitoring and war-room discussions around the clock, the stuff of Hollywood movie scenes, is what unfolds during a cyber attack. The reality is, most cyber attacks pass unnoticed. The security operations team (or equivalent third-party partner) triages alerts, manages incidents, and fends off attackers every minute of every day. There are, however, a growing number of cyber attacks that can, and do, reduce organisations to pen and paper; including Travelex, the world's largest foreign-exchange company. At either end of the spectrum, as a board, you must be aware of how your organisation plans to respond.

Simulations are a valuable investment in time and budget, as they create a safe space in which to learn. A few years ago, we were involved in a simulation exercise where a ransomware payment was demanded within four hours and the attacker was actively posting on Twitter about their demands. Key lessons from the simulation included:

- The board and management had not previously discussed and agreed the organisation's position in the event of ransomware.
- With the CEO on planned leave on the day of the simulation, a contingency plan for who would inform the chairperson, and when, was not in place.

- The CIO and CISO were 'looked to' to lead the incident investigation and make decisions, even though there were others who either had the accountability to make the decisions or were able to make them. This is where crisis management and continuity planning need to be led by the accountable executive, and allow the CIO and CISO to focus on protecting information assets.
- One employee had been nominated as part of crisis management and continuity planning to manage communications. Due to the nature of this attack, that was unrealistic, as it comprised monitoring and responding to Twitter feeds, simulated contact from media outlets requesting updates, and critical communication updates to internal staff. This learning informed varied resource models, based on the type of incident.

A simulation run with a government department, which was more technical in nature, demonstrated the impact of a cyber incident when working with third parties. The simulation role-played a malicious party gaining access to a cloud service that housed sensitive government information. The scenario included a leak to the *Australian Financial Review*, causing a story to be published regarding the nature of the data exposed. There was some consistency with lessons from the previous example, along with some other findings:

The incident response plan was out of date and the runsheet checklist didn't flow smoothly through the steps.

Roles and responsibilities were unclear:

Employees and management involved in the simulation looked to the CIO to make all of the decisions, even though there were others involved who had the accountability to make certain decisions.

Although the privacy officer was involved in the simulation, they were not engaged or consulted as the scenario played out as to the impacts of sensitive data being stolen or disclosed.

Some technical employees did not have clarity on their role in the simulation, given these drills are often used for executive and board member benefit. However, the simulation was an opportunity for the executive team to observe what technical staff experience during an incident. This approach was successful and informative by having a broader group reflect on roles and responsibilities.

Without clear plans, processes, and resources, small attacks that go unnoticed can become a reputational and regulatory headache very quickly, and threaten the enterprise, strategic direction, solvency, performance, compliance, and on-going governance. As such, boards are often offered a drill, game, or simulation exercise to test their knowledge of the planned incident response. These exercises are a must for personnel at all levels of the organisation who are involved in the response to a cyber security incident. From technology to legal, from security operations to the board, each stakeholder must know their role when it comes to incident response, and have practiced how their decisions will impact the organisation's resilience to the attack. (More on resilience in element 2.) With that said, planning for the worst at board level takes more than a tabletop exercise once per year. While these drills are good to bring cyber back to the table and to the forefront of directors' minds, they are only valuable if they have clear objectives, lessons are noted, and actions are taken to change processes and behaviours in case of emergency. They are certainly worth undertaking in light of the IBM Cost of a Data Breach Report 2020, which indicates that incident response testing can bear a major impact on reducing the cost (and effect) of a data breach.[48]

Outside of tabletop exercises, there are steps that boards can take to increase their knowledge and effectiveness in the face of a cyber attack. Firstly, understanding if your organisation has an up-to-date, endorsed cyber-security-incident response plan. A recent survey suggest that more than two thirds of not-for-profits do not have a cyber-security-incident response plan in place, and yet a fifth of charities came under cyber attack in the past 12 months.[49] An essential step in incident response is having a plan to begin with. Having said that, they need to be of high quality, reviewed regularly, and be actionable. The cyber-security-incident response plan is a document that is often too long and gathers dust on a shelf, or is hidden away in a file share. When it comes to incident response, actions are often intuitive, rapid, and, hopefully, collaborative to the extent that a committee decision won't slow down the response. This being the case, it would be rare for a CISO to open up a long-winded response plan and follow it to the letter. Despite lacking regular review or updates, incident response plans do have their place. These documents should lay out incident checklists, contact details of key stakeholders, management escalation paths, internal and external communications advice, and 'playbooks' as to how the organisation has agreed to respond to particular attacks. Cyber-incident response plans must include recovery measures and plans, not just steps to resolve the incident. The restoration of confidence in the organisation's controls and ability to protect against future attack is key for both the board's next steps and in managing customer attrition in response to the incident. Cyber-incident response plans should, also, always include a briefing to the board, both during and post-incident, noting when to call on the board for decisions, and/or post-incident, when lessons have been learned and remediation support may be sought.

Secondly, ideally, discussion and questions regarding incident response should be asked long before you face a crisis. If you were to experience ransomware for example, how would you expect your organisation to recover, and how quickly? Are you in agreement about whether or not you would pay a ransom? If you are not yet in agreement about paying ransoms, now is a good time to raise this with your peers around the boardroom table, along with the CISO, as the occurrence of ransomware attacks is ever-increasing. CISOs are often the victims of bringing forward items 'for noting' or 'for discussion' to the board and, therefore, end up at the back of the agenda, with the paper taken 'as read'. During board meetings a decision is not always sought on cyber, but there is important information to share. There can be great value drawn from dedicated board sessions to bring together board members and security leaders to discuss risk, incident response, and strategic pathways. Empowering the organisation to carry out incident response with the knowledge that the board is aware and in agreement with how response efforts are undertaken and managed can mean vital time is saved not having to seek board-level guidance in the face of a crisis. Remember that every board you are on differs in its approach to cyber security and incident response. While there are similarities, one size does not fit all. Organisations must build incident response plans and capabilities that address the unique risks to your organisation. As a board member, you must have confidence that these plans and capabilities will be sufficient, should they be invoked. See the end of this element for more questions you can ask before, during, and/ or after an incident has occurred.

Finally, making a concerted effort to increase knowledge and awareness is key for directors, as regulators will look to boards first for answers when a cyber attack occurs. Responsibility for cyber in regulated industries such as financial services is more acute than ever. The landscape in Australia is changing, and the need for 'top-down' cyber security governance is increasing. At the time of writing, the Australian Federal Government has recently released their Cyber Security Strategy 2020, but has not yet implemented the frameworks. The strategy, as part of their regulatory agenda, does discuss potential reform to directors' duties relating to cyber security. While the government has not provided the finer details on this reform as yet, those financial services organisations regulated by the APRA Prudential Standard 234 are already well aware of the specific requirements placed on their boards. Notably, APRA expressly provides that boards be ultimately responsible for the information security of the entity; and that the board must ensure the entity maintains information security in a manner commensurate with the size and extent of threats to its information assets, and which enables the continued sound operation of the entity.[50] Should other industries follow suit, they will be exposed to similar repercussions from regulators, such as penalties for non-compliance.

Recovery

In 2020, the average cost of a data breach incident was the best part of AU\$4 million, and almost half of this was incurred more than a year after the incident.[51] Long before this money is spent, organisations take an average of 280 days to identify and respond to an incident. The damage that can be caused by malicious third parties during this time can take years to mop up, and may never be truly quantified. Sometimes, the recovery can be more difficult to manage, and longer lasting, than the incident itself. Organisations can take weeks, months, or may even never recover fully, financially and technically. Logistics company Toll reported nine months after their initial cyber attack in February 2020 that they were still mopping up, including managing regulatory obligations and on-going customer concerns. The case of Toll, and many others, are good opportunities for businesses to learn from others' mistakes. These days, incidents are widely reported in the media and, often, spokespeople will share a version of events with the public. Your CISO should be able to reflect, if appropriate, on your organisation's ability to respond to similar incidents and the controls you have in place, to an extent, that may protect you in similar circumstances.

In the case that you have been breached, how, as a board, can you be sure that the organisation is out of the woods? And that an incident won't occur again? All major cyber incidents should be subject to a post incident review (PIR) and they should be conducted promptly after the incident is completely over. This can be conducted by internal staff, or by a third party if there are many stakeholders involved, both internally and externally. The purpose of a post incident review is to assess the incident response process and the recovery effort in relation to the entire incident, including the root cause. The PIR includes an opportunity to:

- walk through the incident, step by step, to understand the people and processes that were impacted. Did they work as they should?
- document the chronology of events and whether any part of the timing impacted the incident (i.e., delayed response). Was the incident response plan followed to the letter? And did it stand up to the process required?
- document what happened before, during and after the incident.
- dismiss any conflicting stories about how the incident occurred and was managed.
- learn from the incident in the interest of prevention.
- look at actions that worked well.
- review the incident response plan, and include any lessons learned or edit to reflect better practices discovered through the live incident response process you have just undertaken.
- review the technical controls that failed or held strong during an attack.
- consider the personnel involved in the incident, and adjust appropriately.
- gauge, overall, how your response can be improved.

The information provided to the board post incident should work to provide you with confidence that your organisation is safe from a repeat or similar attack. You need to understand:

- the incident itself, before you can focus on whether you are comfortable with the remediation efforts.
- the current and any perceived future business impact.
- the root cause and the reason this exposure was present.
- the response process, in brief.

- how the CISO is incorporating the 'teaching moments' into your company processes.
- the cost of the incident and the clean-up.
- whether you, as a business, were aware of the vulnerability and if it could have been avoided/prevented.
- whether you are liable for the incident and open to lawsuits.

The above can also be used when reflecting on incidents that other organisations have been subject to. With a post-incident mindset, reflecting on how your business may have fared in a similar situation can be helpful in planning and response efforts with your CISO.

Consideration for the board skills matrix

There are board members we spoke to who take the position that cyber is simply one part of the board skills matrix, that you need 'someone' with a legal background, and 'someone' who is technical, and 'someone' who understands cyber. There are many challenges to this way of thinking, but there are two we will raise here.

Firstly, cyber is not a skill that directors should call on in the shape of an expert each time they need security advice from a peer director or a third party. Let us qualify that in saying that the journey to understanding cyber is a long one, and that time with the CISO and third-party experts may certainly be needed in the early days of maturation. Also, we are strong advocates for on-going education. What we hope to convey here is that, for decades, more than a century even, directors were chosen because they all came with finance backgrounds, some also with legal and risk, and these skills saw them through to meet their fiduciary obligations. They kept the ship steady; they understood how to find the risks of insolvency, how to assess risk within the grey areas of the law, and they saw risks as opportunities as much as threats. This is by no means simply history. We still require these skills in spades. What we are saying is that, these days, there are additional lenses through which directors must see the world. All directors must be able to make risk-based decisions when it comes to cyber security, and not look to one or two directors who have dealt with cyber security incidents or issues in the past so they call on their battle scars to assess each CISO's call for investment. True education on what security and technology means now, and is going to mean in the years to come while you continue to take a director's seat, is vital.

Secondly, while the number is growing, there are not that many experienced directors out there who are skilled in cyber. This skill set for boards is a growing need. Cyber as an industry, while not a young industry per se, has not been around as long as lawyers, accountants, and auditors. A professional who is late enough in their career to be looking at a board portfolio career and has a depth of cyber knowledge to apply at board level is not all that common. The number is increasing, and an option to increase this further is to welcome these experts onto your technology committee (if you're fortunate enough to have one), or your audit and risk committee. They may not be as experienced as a director or committee member as some of their peers, but their subject matter expertise, and some carefully selected board training, will allow them to contribute an incredible amount. It will also help to groom the directors of tomorrow. This is something to consider while the board increases their skills. To have opportunities for cyber security leaders to increase their skills as committee members would make a big difference to the boards of the future.

Boards, and audit and risk committees, are experiencing a rise in non-financial risks. For directors this will lead to you seeing a broader range of management of, and providing oversight of, non-financial risk appetites, risk management, and measurement. As a result, there must be consideration to the emerging skills matrix. It is certainly not an easy task to find space on every board for fresh skills. It goes without saying that there are a limited number of seats around the boardroom table, and there are certainly skill sets that cannot be compromised. There is a growing need for cyber to be part of the skills matrix. Technically literate directors, and those with a healthy curiosity and understanding of cyber, are key to the future of organisations. This is not a wasted seat, but one that remains empty, all too often.

Key lessons and reflections

In the event of an incident that requires board involvement, you are safe to assume it has, or could have, a significant impact on operations, finances, and/or customer trust. Crisis management and business continuity planning could also have been involved in the incident, depending on the scope and magnitude. Like crisis management and continuity planning, preparation for cyber incidents is key – you can never be over-prepared. And in the wake of an incident, dedicate time on the board agenda to understand what was learnt: what went well, what should be modified in plans and processes, and what went wrong. This will help you plan for future prevention and resilience. With the changing threats, any confidence you gain from drills, audits, and pre- and post-incident discussions are valuable, remembering that on-going learning and risk assessment is a must.

In the midst of a crisis, you can apply the principles and knowledge you have gained to date to make decisions and draw on your trusted relationships with the CISO and your advisors. The entire board must be ready and willing to be part of preparation, response, and recovery efforts in relation to cyber incidents and on-going risk management.

Areas for reflection

- Are board peers relied on to attest to the cyber risk of your organisation?
- Could you, hand on heart, set the cyber risk appetite and understand the impact of this appetite on cyber spend and the cyber security resources within your organisation?

Questions to ask during a board meeting

- What are our critical information assets?
- Are there clear policies and procedures in place, in the event of an incident?
- If we have run a simulation, what did we learn? How often will we run them? What scenarios will be simulated? How are they chosen?
- Have we established an incident-response team, and which stakeholders are involved?
- How did the incident occur?
- Are we confident we are in a position to prevent the incident from happening again?
- What are our plans, should a key third party fall victim to a cyber attack?
- In the event of an incident, will there be a public announcement?
- In the event of an incident, will a communication be sent to customers?
- Under which circumstances would the police become involved?
- What are our regulatory reporting requirements in relation to an incident?
- What potential threats keep you (the CISO) awake at night?
- Does the executive have a clear and consistent understanding of cyber security relative to their business unit and the enterprise?
- Will a third party be engaged to assist with recovering from the attack or to investigate how the incident occurred? If so, will they share progress reports with the board?

ELEMENT 3

CREATING A CYBER-SAFE BUSINESS WITH A CYBER SECURITY STRATEGY

'Change is the law of life and those who look only to the past or present are certain to miss the future.'

John F. Kennedy

A strategy allows an organisation to be proactive, rather than reactive. Steve Jobs said, 'Focus is about saying no'.[52] An effective strategy provides the ability to say no.

As a board member, there will be elements of any strategy that you seek to review prior to approval and investment. Consider what you look for in a business strategy, a marketing strategy, or an investment strategy, for example. Your approach to a cyber security strategy should follow the same line of understanding, challenge, and alignment. Whilst it may be technical in nature, the cyber security strategy must provide context to the business – customer, risk, compliance – and clearly articulate **what will be different**, once the strategy has been implemented. This can be shown through measurement – there must be a demonstrable improvement in maturity in metrics and measurement in line with investment. (We explore this further in element 4.) The important distinction with a cyber security strategy is that the threats and opportunities shift each day, not dissimilar to an investment strategy. The cyber security strategy, and roadmap, should be revisited and refreshed annually. In Deloitte's 2020 research, the overall cyber security strategy was of interest for 95% of board and management teams.[53] This supports our research, with 91% of directors stating that a clearly defined cyber security strategy is very important to them.

Cyber security is a core component of the business strategy, and if you are not seeing this in your business, there is a gap to address. An effective cyber security strategy will establish a clear connection to the business strategy. The business strategy will inform aspects of the cyber security strategy relating to existing strengths, growth aspirations, business threats, and weaknesses. The cyber security strategy must comprise elements of protection across *the security collective*. We would expect the cyber security strategy to be a three-year strategy, as a five-year strategy for an area that changes so rapidly would be challenged to remain relevant.

Investment in the execution of a cyber security strategy could be both substantial and significant. As a board, it is imperative that you are engaged and informed throughout this process, and for management to demonstrate a level of understanding, consideration, and recommendation before you are asked to endorse or approve the strategy. Has management clearly articulated what will be different, once the strategy has been implemented? What did not make it into the strategy, and why? Was the decision financial? Will this have an impact on risk?

Through our study for this book, directors shared the following evidence that they look for prior to endorsing cyber-related investment decisions. This element explores these topics and more. Directors want to see:

- a cyber security strategy designed to address risk and protect against emerging threats
- displayed business and commercial acumen to inform the planning, sequencing, and implementation of cyber initiatives
- existing capability assessed against industry best practice

- demonstrated project management expertise and that governance is, or will be, established for these important projects
- consideration for how effectiveness of the strategy will be measured through evaluation of risk, assessment against a framework, a shift in metrics, and/or third-party assurance

Elements of a comprehensive cyber security strategy

'The board needs to trust that senior management has a long-term view of cybersecurity, with a strategic road map and plans in place to adequately protect information assets and IT systems, regardless of where and how new threats emerge.' [54]

Through your executive and board career you will become familiar with both good and great strategies. The components you expect to find in any business strategy are the same for a cyber security strategy. Management can be considered to have done a great job when they share a strategy with a supporting board paper which has pre-empted your questions and answered them. In our research with CISOs, 100% said that having the board's endorsement of the cyber security strategy is very important to them. Due to the unique nature of the cyber security strategy, and the pace of emerging risk, let's discuss the eight essential elements of an all-inclusive cyber strategy.

1. An assessment of the organisation's current threat landscape, including culture, systems, processes, audit findings, risk profile, and vendor partnerships. This may be approached in two ways:

(a) Utilising a cyber security framework, for example, National Institute of Standards and Technology (NIST) or International Standards Organisation (ISO), to measure the assessment against an industry model. This can be an effective way of measuring the return on investment – the improvement to the maturity of cyber security measures – as the strategy is implemented, which also reduces the risk exposure. If this is the path taken, then a target maturity should be set as part of measuring the effectiveness of the implementation of the strategy. A target maturity rating, like the risk-appetite statement, has cost implications. Therefore, the target – or aspirational target – maturity rating must be established as part of the strategy development. Organisations do not need to achieve 100% maturity in all aspects of security. We have seen risk reduction effectively evaluated against NIST maturity, i.e., attaching an existing 'weighting' against each risk and setting a target increase in maturity.

(b) Undertaking a SWOT analysis (a strategic-planning technique to identify strengths, weaknesses, opportunities, and threats related to cyber security) to provide clarity on what needs to be solved. While this is an effective approach, and familiar to most professionals, it does not measure the maturity (which may inform prioritisation). Furthermore, it relies on the experience and expertise of the individuals undertaking the assessment (creating a risk that something may be missed) and does not provide the ability to measure improvement. In this instance, risk reduction may be evaluated through a self appraisal.

2. External benchmarks to provide perspective on security performance compared to others, investment in security initiatives, and team-size comparisons. Although there are benefits to specify the comparison to organisations in the same industry as your own, with cyber security, the threats are the same for all organisations, and a broad approach to benchmarking can be valuable to create a standard. Having both worked in Financial Services, we have experienced

aspirations to have the cyber maturity of the top four banks. For many Financial Service organisations, the investment, in systems and people, is out of reach. Using the top four banks as an example, the benefit of benchmarking them is to understand the current maturity level and how they got there. This may create an opportunity for step change, rather than incremental change, which achieves maturity aspirations in a more cost-effective way.

3. High-level strategic objectives will be established through the SWOT analysis and/or maturity benchmarking exercise. These objectives must represent *the security collective* and be a set of statements that articulate the strategic goals for the organisation. Ideally, due to the technical nature of cyber and the critical role we all play in keeping the organisation safe, these should be meaningful and memorable to all employees. To assist with creating broad understanding and buy-in, these strategic objectives should connect into the business strategy. This is best achieved through the development of a Strategic Alignment Framework, usually developed by the PMO, which will effectively align business ideas and initiatives to the business strategy. This not only supports project prioritisation but also benefits realisation.

4. A set of guiding principles to inform prioritisation, sequencing, investment, and decision making. These guiding principles relate to the development and implementation of the strategy – they are not cyber security guiding principles – therefore, you should expect them to be business-focussed, rather than technical in nature. We recommend four to six guiding principles which should include the name, a one-line summary of the intent of the principle, describe the principle in a way which is meaningful for everyone involved in the work – we have found approaching these through detailed

'new ways of thinking and working' statements are effective –and achieve the desired outcome. For example:

(a) Name of guiding principle: Cyber protection with partners

(b) Principle summary: We only partner with organisations that meet our minimum standards of protection for critical information assets

(c) Ways of thinking and working: Data sovereignty will be part of the selection criteria for all procurement activities (RFx). This will result in vendors that cannot meet our data sovereignty standards either not responding or submitting a non-compliant response. We will benefit from this principle by avoiding lengthy commercial negotiations and assist with managing risk within appetite.

Each architecture, project, and business decision that is made will anchor to the set of guiding principles. While not all decisions will comply with this principle, the board or sub-committee should be made aware of decisions made outside of these guidelines.

5. A roadmap to inform the implementation of the strategy will reflect a number of inputs, including the most critical risk(s) to be minimised, areas of priority for maturity uplift, and a sequence which is designed holistically for a no-regrets approach to change and investment. It is imperative that the roadmap is developed in line with the organisation's ability to deliver and consume change, the annual funding available, and what percentage of the portfolio the business will allocate to cyber. Often, it may be appealing to allocate a large portion of funding to cyber security with the intent to reduce risk through this investment. This approach may result in an imbalance between cyber tools and processes

and the cyber culture and behaviours to achieve the initial, and critical, business imperative to protect information. In our experience, this does not achieve the desired outcomes, as the business is challenged to: a) deliver that amount of change, b) consume the intended business benefits of change, and c) develop a security culture at the same pace as the implementation of systems and processes.

6. Describe – in depth – what will be different as the strategy is implemented. We would expect management to share this detail for the annual investment and delivery cycle of the strategy. This can be a challenging task for management, as tangible outcomes must be demonstrated. As a board, we need to acknowledge that business cases have not yet been developed and project schedules not defined, so allow for some leeway, although management must communicate any changes to you to manage expectations. 'What will be different' will be inclusive of *the security collective* and measurable wherever possible, with some examples including:

(a) Enterprise cyber security risk rating minimised from Extreme to High (or rating A to B, depending on your organisation's terminology), bringing it within the risk appetite

(b) Automated management of employee access to systems (through resignation or change of job responsibilities) to reduce risk of access to sensitive information, and removal of the manual process to manage this, will address a recurring audit finding

(c) Through employee education, the response to simulated phishing attacks as a way to test employee awareness and understanding is reduced from 30% of staff who click on the suspect link to 5%

(d) Cyber attacks identified and blocked 95% of the time, an increase from 70% through partnering with a 24x7 managed service security provider with sophisticated monitoring and global insights to new attacks

The return on an investment into *the security collective* capabilities is often not evidenced until there is an incident or a near miss. This is unlike the return on a tangible investment like property or equipment. For example, much of what security relies upon is the commitment to processes and governance to make controls effective. This is an important part of security culture. Often, it is when these controls break down that the return on investment into technical detection and prevention can be realised.

7. An investment case to implement the strategy. Detailed business cases will be created as part of the project initiation phase. At the time of the strategy being shared with the board for approval, you can expect an investment case to be shared. An investment case aligns the estimated project costs, by year, with the roadmap. Management includes assumptions made and risks to the detailed planning and execution of the strategy. The investment case needs to allow for an order of magnitude in cost estimates. The order-of-magnitude thresholds are usually defined by the Enterprise Program Management Office (ePMO). The ePMO should be actively involved in the development of the investment case.

8. Following the board's approval of the strategy, management will commence planning. Management should share these planning activities at a high level in the board paper or strategy pack. We would expect them to include:

(a) A communications plan to socialise the approved strategy with stakeholders, including all employees, regulators, auditors, the risk team, and shared services like procurement and human resources, where support to implement the strategy will be required

(b) Definition of the Cyber Security team structure and operating model – the CIO and CISO design an organisation structure and operating model to enable the implementation of the strategy

(c) Integration of the Year 1 roadmap initiatives into ePMO planning and funding allocation, and definition of how the delivery will be governed

(d) The timing of the next update to the board, and what you should expect to see

Independent assurance for greater confidence

Many boards and CEOs gain comfort through third-party due diligence, particularly when it comes to IT, as the risk exposures are significant, investment is high, and missteps can be costly. Engaging an assurance partner to review the cyber security strategy is becoming more common. In the experience of CIOs and CISOs, our research shows that boards gain increased confidence through third-party-partner due diligence, from assurance of risk ratings and benchmarking of industry peers, assessment of strategic objectives, and associated initiatives, to validation of the roadmap and reporting.

Embarking on third-party assurance requires investment. It is important to understand how this will be funded. If the funding has not been provisioned through the internal audit plan, we encourage you to understand if it will be funded by the allocation of funds to the cyber strategy, as this may result in important investment being directed to a review over important risk mitigation or capability uplift initiatives.

When engaging a third party to review the strategy, it is important to understand that we are engaging them for their point of view through experience, expertise, global network, and research. We should not expect a clear appraisal. This does not mean that the strategy is not appropriate for the organisation – it is providing a different perspective, which will warrant a discussion at board level or in a sub-committee. Your CEO, CIO, and CISO have a deep understanding of the business, and engaging them for their perspective on the findings and recommendations at the board meeting will be valuable. In this instance, supporting the assurance party over management may dilute trust and morale.

The recommendations from the review, along with management insights and comments, may result in modifications to the strategy or roadmap. Often, any decisions resulting from an assurance review will need to be assessed against the broader business context. This context includes business and security landscape, security threats, security current state, risk appetite, availability of budget, and trade-offs against other priority initiatives.

Successful strategy execution

Once the strategy has been approved, the board should expect visibility into how management will govern the implementation of the strategy, and how often the board will receive progress updates. This governance conversation may be at the same board meeting where strategy approval is sought, or at the following meeting, depending on the time allocation on the agenda. Our preference is to separate these topics, providing that the following board meeting is within four to eight weeks, as both require lengthy understanding and discussion.

Most ePMOs have clearly defined and documented methods to plan and govern projects, including resource requirements, risk identification and management, benefits realisation, and how to develop a sourcing approach in collaboration with the procurement team. At a high level, these topics should be shared with the board for transparency.

There are several ways to govern the implementation of the Cyber Security roadmap, and some organisations implement a hybrid:

Management governance – through a steering committee or project board. The board should understand who the members of this forum are, why they have been selected, and how often they meet.

Board governance – by management providing status updates to the board or a sub-committee; for example, the audit and risk committee. It is becoming favoured to establish a board sub-committee, such as a technology advisory committee, digital committee, or technology & projects committee, with a focus on IT, including data, digital, cyber, artificial intelligence (AI), and legacy systems. This approach provides the opportunity to engage independent directors to supplement the skills matrix with backgrounds in IT, strategic projects, transformation, and/ or risk.

Third-party assurance – requested by the board or proposed by management, third-party assurance is an effective governance method. This is a productive approach when the assurance partner has participated in the development or due diligence of the cyber security strategy.

The design of the governance model should consider:

- Relativity to the estimated whole-of-life cost to implement the initiatives
- Complexity of the governance model itself – the cost; will the board and/or management receive the same status updates from multiple sources; and could it confuse stakeholders or blur accountabilities?

- Possibility of management investing more time in reporting rather than delivering

The quality of governance is dependent on relevant tools, appropriate resourcing, and the model itself – if it is not meeting the intended outcomes, or is insufficient, how is this addressed? Governance is often seen as a hygiene factor, rather than business critical. Not having the right governance model, tools, and resourcing in place puts the execution of the strategy at risk.

It is imperative that the board set the expectation with management that the board expect to hear bad news as soon as possible. Depending on the severity, this can be facilitated through a phone call between the chairperson and CEO, an email or out-of-cycle board paper shared digitally with board members, or an update at the next board meeting.

Strategic partnerships

With the volume of cyber-related change initiatives, operational activities, and a global skills shortage, the reality is that we rely on strategic partnerships to meet expectations and growing demands. Strategic partnering is a valuable method to gain access to expertise, efficiency, and economies of scale.

A great example is the ability for management to monitor business activity 24x7 to identify and respond to potential and real cyber threats by using skilled third-party expert partners. Mobilising this capability internally requires an increase in headcount and budget, and investment in the required tools. In the event that these are not constraints for the business, there is also value in gaining global insights from a reputable service provider. Putting a strategic partnership in place to monitor for threats, triage events, and manage the resolution of incidents, or hand the incident to the client to rectify, is an approach that is scalable, sustainable, and should provide global visibility and insights. Such decisions should be considered as part of the implementation of the cyber strategy.

From a board perspective, it is important to understand the size and expertise of the organisation's internal cyber security team and vendor relationships: Does that information correlate with your expectations on coverage, responsiveness, and scalability? You need reassurance that sufficient 24x7 monitoring and an incident response capability is in place, either internally or with a third-party partner. It is also worth understanding if management has a plan in place in the event that the organisation experiences multiple cyber incidents concurrently, or if an incident ran for weeks or months around the clock.

Cyber insurance

The Secure Board would not be complete without a note about cyber insurance. As you might imagine, what follows should be considered general information and not construed as advice.

What could be seen by boards as one of the most important strategic partnerships is that of the organisation and their cyber insurance provider, despite the number of organisations with dedicated cyber policies remaining modest. Cyber insurance has grown in popularity over the past decade or so, and we certainly understand how the board can grasp this topic, given their knowledge and understanding of the importance of investing in other insurance products. As a specific specialty insurance policy, cyber insurance is intended to support organisations to respond and recover from a cyber incident. Acknowledging that prevention and risk minimisation are key cyber-strategic objectives, an organisation also needs to consider the resources and actions available, should prevention strategies fail. While cyber insurance can provide peace of mind to boards and organisations that there is some financial support to reduce the impact in the wake of a cyber incident, insurance alone cannot reduce the likelihood or potential long-term trust implications of a cyber incident (both of which have been discussed in earlier elements).

The number of cyber insurance claims has steadily risen over the last few years, from 77 claims in 2016, when cyber was still a relatively new line of insurance, to 809 in 2019. In 2020, there were already 770 claims in the first three quarters. This steady increase in claims has been driven, in part, by the growth of the global cyber-insurance market, which is currently estimated to be worth US$7 billion.[55] This rise in claims will certainly have an impact on premiums, and also the types of claims that can be made.

In terms of pros and cons for cyber insurance, the list below, while not exhaustive, may be of help.

Pros

- The work done by insurance companies could improve and redefine security standards.
- Financial incentives to improve IT security: better insurance coverage at lower rates could become a possibility if you uplift security measures and lower risk.
- Greater executive awareness: recognising the scope of cyber risks and the severity of their consequences could pave the way for much-needed security initiatives.

Cons

- Smaller companies may not keep pace: if a business operates with a more modest budget, they may not have the funds necessary for insurance, a disadvantage compared to large corporations.
- A false sense of security: after obtaining insurance, businesses may not put in enough effort into developing policies and investing in their security.
- Investing in insurance cannot prevent a cyber attack in the same way that funding can be applied to other prevention activities.

At the end of the day, cyber insurance can form part of your risk treatment plans to transfer risk away from your organisation. However, you cannot transfer all risk, and many claims are made to insurers for incidents caused by human error, which is the most difficult cause of cyber risk to mitigate and minimise. Many insurers offer products and services pre-breach that will support your organisation to put frameworks and structure in place that will help you be resilient to cyber attack. Insurance, though, is not a silver bullet, and relies heavily on the insurance company being provided accurate, up-to-date information in order for risks to be quantified. For many enterprises, only the CFO or senior finance and risk professionals have the expertise to properly assess the value of cyber insurance investments, the total cost of an incident, and, therefore, the potential return of investment of the insurance policy.

The board's role relating to the cyber security strategy

In addition to the board's fiduciary and regulatory requirements, during our research with CIOs and CISOs we gathered valuable insights into management's perspective on the important role the board plays in relation to the cyber security strategy. We share these verbatim comments for your consideration:

'It is imperative for the board to endorse the security strategy. It assists them in understanding the why, and better understand the risk, as well as the funding required. Also, for the board to understand, if funding is not approved, what the consequential risk is.'

'It's essential that an organisation has a cyber security strategy, particularly one endorsed by, visible to, and progress reported on to the board. It helps me do my job, because with an appropriately endorsed strategy investment, decisions that flow out of it are already "pre-endorsed" and don't need debating at each and every budget season. It's also helpful to manage the board's expectation about the evolution of cyber security, particularly when it evolves from a lower base.'

In our research, a CIO shared this: 'The challenge is to ensure that security doesn't become a compliance matter for the board'.

Key lessons and reflections

It is imperative that the cyber security strategy provide business context to the board. The cyber strategy must align with the business strategy and describe what will be different in business outcomes. Often, the benefits of implementing the cyber strategy are not fully realised until there is a breach or near miss. In the event of a breakdown in controls, it is often the investment in detection and prevention that keep the information assets safe.

We can expect external partners to contribute to the cyber strategy, security operations, and more. The expertise of a strategic partner may be sought to facilitate the development of the cyber security strategy, an independent review of the strategy, or assurance throughout the implementation of the strategy. Partnerships are also established to provide expertise, tools, and scale to the operations of your cyber function. From a risk perspective, one such partnership is that of an insurer. Boards are faced with the cyber insurance discussion more and more these days, and it is not a decision to be made lightly.

Currency of the cyber strategy is a challenge for every organisation. With the threat landscape constantly changing, we recommend that the strategy and implementation roadmap is revisited and refreshed annually or when events occur that may trigger a review, such as a change in business structure, a revised business strategy, a revised IT strategy or even a new CISO. There are some cases when you may need to revisit the strategy out of the standard cycle. This review may result in an update to the strategy and/or inform a reprioritisation of the implementation sequence as prescribed in the roadmap. Whether you are presented with a new, existing, or refreshed strategy, the CISO must bring to your attention what will be different, once the strategy has been delivered, to assist you to understand the impact of your investment.

Areas for reflection

- Would third-party assurance of the strategy provide me with a higher level of comfort?
- Is management demonstrating an understanding and commitment to the cyber security strategy? (This may be through reference to the strategy from the CRO or function/ resource allocation.)

Questions to ask during a board meeting

- Who owns the execution of the strategy?
- Why are these initiatives required now?
- How will the strategy ensure that we meet our compliance requirements?
- Is it a risk-led roadmap?
- What's not in the strategy? Why?
- Is it future-proof? How will we be future-proof?
- How have you, as CISO, prioritised the investments?
- How is investment allocated to high-risk scenarios?
- What about compliance obligations?
- How will we resource this strategy?
- If you, as CISO, had more money/resources, etc., could you implement sooner?
- How will you, as CISO, and the CIO ensure the strategy remains current?

ELEMENT 4

MEANINGFUL METRICS, MEASUREMENT, AND REPORTING

'Gartner clients are also reporting that after years of quarterly reporting on cybersecurity to their boards, that boards are now pushing back and asking for improved data and understanding of what they have achieved after years of such heavy investment.'

Gartner, 'The Urgency to Treat Cybersecurity As a Business Decision', 2020

While other functional management reports to the board remain static (financial reporting is a good example), you should expect the cyber metrics to mature as the business matures through the implementation of the strategy, and as employee education and awareness improves. Reporting enables you to govern cyber risk against appetite, assess the culture through a security lens, should prompt a board discussion on reputational risk in the event of a cyber incident, and provoke a dialogue on how your organisation would fare against an incident similar to one that another organisation has experienced. Management reports must provide you with visibility to the most business-critical aspects of cyber security for the business. Meaningful cyber security reporting must provide you with valuable insights far beyond the metrics themselves.

What 'good' looks like

A methodical approach to developing cyber reporting for the board aligns measures and metrics with the business strategy, company scorecard, risk-appetite statements, and regulation. This approach creates continuity for the board, as it connects cyber activities to other corporate artefacts that you are familiar with, and helps management establish a clear narrative. Well considered board reports represent all aspects of cyber, including:

- progress against strategy
- security operations – preventing, detecting, analysing, and responding to incidents,
- risk management
- employee, partner and customer awareness
- security patching
- activities to address audit findings and penetration tests

While these measures are fairly standard, the actual metrics vary, depending on the business; for example, the industry, risk appetite, and regulation.

If your business is initiating cyber metrics for the first time, expect a few iterations. This may feel operational in nature, and tedious. An effective way to establish board reporting is to have a board sub-committee work through iterations with management prior to the final report coming to the board. During our research for this book, we spoke with a number of self-professed 'bean counters' who, as directors, rely on management to provide the data and analysis for them to gain comfort. For cyber, that will often require the CISO/CIO/CEO to understand the data and analysis the board needs to see to meet its fiduciary obligations, and a sense of comfort that reporting covers strategy, operations, and culture. We suggest that management share an initial report to gain feedback from the board or sub-committee. Once agreed, management must continue to produce regular reports as good practice and only report on exceptions to the board. Detailed cyber reports can be provided to the board as an appendix, if preferred. The key insights, or 'what to look for', from cyber board reporting include:

Threats: represents the volume of external threats and how many have been blocked. Historical data is valuable here for you to identify if threats are stable or increasing, and management's on-going ability to identify and block threats. If a third-party vendor is accountable for threat detection, this information can also be beneficial for vendor performance management.

Incident response and resolution: once an incident has been detected, it is important to measure and report on the time it takes management to respond to, and resolve, an incident. Historical data provides useful insights. Reporting should be by criticality of the incident (critical high, medium, low) for which management needs to provide a definition.

Prevention, including cyber culture: understanding the risk in the existing business landscape and management's plans to remediate are extremely important. Where important remediation work is unfunded or not resourced, this is an opportunity for the board to influence the severity of this work. The important item to seek and understand in prevention reporting is vulnerabilities against the risk appetite; for example, adherence of security patching to tolerance levels; level of unauthorised cloud services in use (as mentioned in element 2). Employee engagement and understanding can be measured by cyber-awareness-training completion rates and the results of phishing simulations.

Status updates: management reporting must include progress of milestones against implementation of cyber strategy, including benefits realisation, the root cause of past incidents and remediation plans following a full investigation process, compliance and governance, and emerging issues, including new cyber threats and learning from other organisations that have experienced an incident.

Valuable insights beyond the metrics

- Metrics should evolve to represent emerging threats along with the improved performance of the business as the cyber strategy is implemented
- The CIO or CISO can demonstrate awareness and an appetite to learn from others by sharing details of incidents experienced by other organisations; it is useful to hear of the incidents and the 'near misses'
- Metrics should demonstrate the return on investment relating to the implementation of the strategy or a strategic partnership put in place; for example, a managed security service provider
- Phishing exercises are most valuable with current and historical data to identify trends and gain insights; generally, phishing exercises become more sophisticated, often mimicking a trusted brand, like Australia Post, or an internal email from Human Resources – the level of cyber awareness can be assessed through this lens: How cognisant are employees when a phishing email comes from a trusted brand?
- Cyber security is complex and a critical issue; cyber updates to the board should share successes, near misses, incidents, and lessons; the board play an instrumental role in establishing a learning culture
- Storytelling is an art form; the CISO needs to share the story in business terms to measure finance, risk, culture, and strategy with trends, targets, and metrics to support the narrative and the importance of their function – the cyber narrative for the board, backed by evidence, is impactful

- Directing an appropriate cyber question to the CEO rather than the CIO or CISO provides insight into the level of executive understanding and engagement in security
- Historical trend reporting demonstrates how the security team is functioning over time, helping you to understand what is working and what areas are deteriorating
- A security incident that is detected but not blocked is a control failure – this unforeseen risk should be discussed, understood, and the root cause mitigated

Measuring maturity through industry frameworks

Industry frameworks are a useful way to measure cyber security maturity and gain insights. While our research shows that only 50% of board members rely on a cyber security framework to measure maturity and progress, understanding that several frameworks exist, and the value of them, is an important component of governing cyber security. This standardised approach to measuring maturity assists in validating the progress made as the strategy is implemented, while highlighting areas that may require focus. The board should not expect the assessment to provide a 'clear' report card. The value gained is through the insights from the assessment; for example, overall employee engagement in being security conscious, the understanding of cyber security across the organisation, alignment, understanding, and focus areas across IT. You will effectively be able to measure the maturity against execution of the strategy, which is great for visibility to return on investment, and a potentially valuable reference for lowering a cyber security risk rating. Of note: There are security industry frameworks (i.e., NIST) and there are also mandatory regulatory framework requirements. The regulatory frameworks are often based on security maturity principles and standards, with the industry quirks and requirements provided as a contextual overlay. Industry maturity frameworks cannot be underestimated in terms of importance. For example, the Australian Energy Sector Cyber Security Framework has been a work in progress for a number of years, with a huge amount of collaboration across industry stakeholders. What the AESCSF brings, that general frameworks do not, is the governance and benchmarking within the industry. While maturity targets are nice to have in some industries, in others they are mandated and governed, something to consider and learn more about, should you be on the board of a critical infrastructure provider, particularly energy.

How often should cyber be on the board agenda?

'Having an engaged board can help the entire organisation focus on the challenge of managing cyber risk while assuring that adequate resources are allocated. And board oversight should be ongoing, rather than only at the initial stages or when there is a cyber incident.' [56]

Through our research, 77% of directors gain confidence in the organisation being cyber safe through regular board reporting and metrics. IT leaders who participated in our research told us that many report to the board on an annual basis, or as requested. These IT leaders expressed to us that reporting annually is not enough. McKinsey research supports our findings, with only 25% of companies presenting IT security updates to the board more than once a year, and up to 35% of companies reporting this information only on demand.[57]

In our research, when we asked what it means to a CIO for the board to understand cyber security and engage in a meaningful conversation, one shared this: 'My organisation has established an IT-focussed board sub-committee with approximately 40% of the content presented and discussed being cyber-related; with a further audit and risk sub-committee with cyber security agenda items. The elevation of cyber as a critical agenda topic was intentional by the board and management – in part to motivate all staff to consider their actions as part of the control framework rather than compartmentalise it.'

How often cyber is on the board agenda may vary if you govern cyber through the audit and risk committee or a sub-committee which has been established to provide oversight of IT, including digital, data, and AI. We recommend that cyber is reported to the board bi-annually at a minimum, with an agreement that management brings agenda items such as an incident, regulatory change, or third-party breach to the board outside of the agreed schedule.

Emerging threats, evolving metrics

Cyber security threats are continually changing. Metrics, risk assessments, and controls should adapt to these emerging threats. These should be clearly articulated in management reporting and the activities underway or completed to adjust the security posture. The update to the board on emerging threats by the CIO or CISO, and the resulting conversation, will be a valuable discussion. Your CIO and CISO will be aware of global and local emerging threats, and learn from incidents that other organisations experience through their network, industry conferences, podcasts, and media. The CISO community is immensely important to your CISO and the organisation. It should not be undervalued. **Within the trusted CISO community, details of incidents or near misses are shared in strict confidence, which provides the crucial opportunity for others to learn.** These insights make your CISO more effective in their role and valuable to the organisation. You can support them by encouraging networking and helping them grow their network by facilitating introductions to cyber professionals that you meet through your network.

Similarly, as cyber maturity rises for the business through the implementation of the strategy, developing capability, tools and processes, establishing strategic partnerships, and educating employees, the bar should be raised on performance.

The cyber landscape has shifted significantly over the past five years, with cyber crime now costing the global economy US$6 trillion. Years ago we had conversations about how much money was required to provide assurance that information was secure from attacks. Nowadays, the discussion centres on *when* we experience a large-scale cyber incident, rather than *if*. How we identify, respond, and resolve incidents plays a significant role in reputational damage and consumer trust. Some examples of the shift in trends:

- 2015's highest-profile attack was on the adultery site Ashley Madison sharing personal information, including email addresses and home addresses, of 37 million users.
- The greatest bank robbery of the 2000s was a digital attack on 100 banks in 30 countries, hacking into systems to dispense money from ATMs and transfer funds between accounts, totalling $1 billion.
- In 2016, Australia's Blood Bank exposed the personal details of 550,000 donors when a third party that managed the Blood Bank website stored the donor information in an unsecured environment.
- Hackers identified a weakness at a Las Vegas casino in 2017 when they successfully hacked into systems through a high-tech fish tank, located in the foyer, which had unsecured internet connectivity.
- A data breach of Marriott International hotels in 2018 saw the private data of 500,000 customers, including address, credit card, and passport details, exposed.
- My Health Record, the digital health record for Australians, recorded 42 data breaches in 2018.
- Travelex, the world's largest currency exchange, had to shut down their IT systems on New Year's Eve, 2019, after customer data was breached, including dates of birth, credit card information, and national insurance numbers. Media outlets reported that a ransom of between US$3 million and $6 million was demanded to return the data, with an ultimate payment of US$2.3 million. In August 2020, the company announced it would cease trading in the US and Canada,

stating that the cyber attack was a key factor, along with the pandemic.

- At the height of the COVID-19 pandemic, over 500,000 Zoom accounts were stolen and sold on the dark web, which is a part of the internet that allows users to remain anonymous and untraceable.
- In 2016, Uber's data breach exposed the contact details of 57 million customers and drivers. Uber paid the hackers US$100,000 in an attempt to cover up the theft. This poor judgement impacted the organisation's reputation and trust, with the company valuation dropping by US$20 billion.

As a society and as leaders of organisations of all shapes and sizes, we are vulnerable to a cyber attack, now more than ever. The pace with which cyber threats evolve is impossible to predict or keep up with. As such, organisations must continue to move from a tactical, technical approach to strategic cyber-resilience plans. In saying that, even within those organisations with a well-planned cyber strategy, directors face sharp changes in direction as the cyber strategy and metrics are refreshed to reflect both the changing threat landscape, and to proactively address risks that other organisations already face.

Learning from others

In every aspect of our lives we can learn from others, and cyber security is no different. Particularly as cyber threats will continue to evolve, and no amount of funding will provide 100% assurance of being safe. Hackers create new threats at a pace that governments and organisations cannot keep up with. Learning has never been so critical. Ultimately, you want to understand if the organisation is vulnerable to another organisation's cyber incident.

Learning from the other organisations that have experienced a cyber incident – or a 'near miss' – is not constrained by geography, industry, budget, or size. An important component of the CISO role is sharing the experiences of other organisations, undertaking self diagnosis, and sharing lessons and remediation activities with the board. We categorise learning in three areas:

1. Learn from industry peers and case studies – for a number of years hackers focussed their efforts on Australian banks, as they knew work was underway to mature policies, processes, and controls, and if the attack were successful, the available reward was high. We then saw banks invest heavily in protecting against attacks, and the focus of hackers shifted to smaller financial institutions, including superannuation and insurance. This trend is common across all industries. In the event of another organisation experiencing a cyber incident, it is likely that you will hear about the cyber attack through the media, mandated reporting to regulators, or through your network. In our experience, the most valuable lessons will derive from the relationship your CISO has with security peers, regardless of industry. Through these relationships, your CISO will be able to understand how the incident occurred, what led to it being detected, given that the average time taken to identify an incident such as a data breach is 280 days,[58] the organisation's response to customers, employees, shareholders, and regulators, and detail on what action was required to resolve the incident. This may inform new security exposures, and possibly a heightened risk rating, the re-prioritisation of planned initiatives to ensure protection, or uplift in maturity for existing controls. If your CISO does not proactively share these insights with you, we recommend asking for them.

2. Insights from researchers and strategic partners – reputable researchers, like Gartner and MIT, gather and share information on how organisations are improving their security posture and detecting cyber exposures and threats more quickly. Research papers and insights provide the

opportunity for reflection, observation, and remediation. Strategic partnerships may be a less obvious source of learning. We have found that true strategic relationships are developed through a mutually beneficial relationship built on trust, not a contract. In our experience, partners, local and global, gain valuable insights through their broad client base and share lessons, while maintaining confidentiality. This is another opportunity to improve threat detection capability, incident response plans, and cyber culture.

3. Assurance through internal and external audit – audit activities are beneficial to gain a different perspective or validate management reporting. We have always found insights from audit activities to be valuable, from annual control testing to regulatory compliance and penetration testing. A penetration test, often referred to as a pen test, is an authorised simulated cyber attack to evaluate security of the systems. It is important to note that the results of a penetration test are only valid at the time of the test. If management addresses the findings several months after the penetration test, this does not mean the organisation is more secure or has no vulnerabilities. New threats and vulnerabilities are created every day. We recommend alternating providers for annual penetration testing, as different providers have varied tools and resources. In our experience, different providers identify differing findings for management to address.

Audit activities can also be useful to validate the effectiveness and benefits realisation of cyber initiatives – the return on investment. If audit findings do not align with management updates, we recommend asking management for their point of view.

Does it matter who provides the cyber update to the board?

For us, the importance of the board having visibility to the CISO and building two-way trust is fundamental. **The CISO holds an extreme level of accountability for the organisation, and professional and personal consequences if things don't go right. We believe it is mutually beneficial to all parties for the board and CISO to connect.**

Like all relationships, your relationship and level of trust with the CISO or security leader will grow over time. It is important to have both in place when decisions need to be made. Imagine if your first interaction with the CISO was during a crisis or incident! Part of the CISO's role is to say no to business leaders – and sometimes that leader will be the CEO – to protect sensitive information, data, and the company brand. They need to know that you have their back.

We acknowledge that cyber is a deeply technical domain. If your CISO is highly technical, it may be tempting to get cyber updates from your CIO. Most likely, your CIO has more experience reporting to the board and can articulate risk mitigation and risk management plans more succinctly, and in business terms. If this is the case for your organisation, we recommend inviting the CISO to attend the board meeting for cyber updates from the CIO and, over time, have the CISO present part of the update.

Often, the chief risk officer reports on business functions or activities on which cyber security is dependent, or vice versa; for example, the classification and governance of data, governance of vendor contracts, or phishing exercises. Management reporting should connect the dots for you on these related activities.

We advocate for the relationship and trust between the board and the CISO to be prioritised over a polished presentation. Developing skills to prepare board papers, present information to the board, and navigate Q&A are areas where training and coaching are available.

Key lessons and reflections

The reporting of metrics, measurements, and insights for cyber security, a non-financial risk, is different to long-standing board reports like Financial Reporting. The board needs a level of comfort that management has the appropriate metrics and measurement in place, although bringing all metrics to the board generally proves unproductive, as the eye is drawn to 'red' reporting items, and important detail could be missed. In the case of metrics, we recommend that management prepare a board report for socialising and feedback, along with a proposed approach to exemption reporting. Board members can then assess the report against the information, data, and insights you look for to meet your fiduciary obligations. Full cyber metrics reporting can be provided as an appendix, if the board prefers.

The other variation to board reporting is that cyber metrics must evolve as the maturity of security and culture improves. We would expect management to advance reporting as the cyber security strategy is implemented. Cyber maturity can also be measured against globally recognised cyber frameworks or industry-specific frameworks.

We recommend that cyber be on the board agenda bi-annually, along with an agreement that management provides the board with relevant updates as required. We encourage boards to have the CISO attend the board meeting to provide the cyber update. If this is an area for development for the CISO, there is formal training available, along with the alternatives to commence with reporting at a board sub-committee or to jointly report with the CIO.

Areas for reflection

- A well-known term in cyber circles is FUD: fear, uncertainty, doubt. Is our CISO or CIO using FUD to gain access to investment or resources?
- What's keeping me awake at night?
- Do I have confidence in the metrics before me?

Questions for your CEO, CIO, or CISO

- Why are we always hearing good news?
- Why are we always hearing bad news?
- What's keeping you awake at night?
- How does this metric/measure relate to business risk and/or the customer?
- How do you assess the delivery of cyber initiatives against the impact to the risk profile?
- As a milestone is delivered, where/when/how will we see this reflected in the metrics?
- Do you have adequate resources – people, budget? If we allocated additional funds, what would the benefit be? If we reduced funding, what impact would it have?

ELEMENT 5

UNDERSTANDING THE ROLE OF THE CISO (AND IF YOU NEED ONE)

'The ultimate measure of a man is not where he stands in moments of comfort and convenience but where he stands in times of challenge and controversy.'

Martin Luther King Jr

In a parallel universe, there is a book for CISOs with a chapter entitled 'Understanding the role of the board', or even a book called *The Board-Ready CISO*. In our experience, while there are many CISOs and boards that exist in harmony, there are also many CISO–board relationships which are disjointed or non-existent. This may be due to a lack of understanding of each other's roles, that the level of influence in each other's worlds is unclear, and/ or that the benefits of building a trusted relationship between the board and their security leader have not been realised.

Through validating whether we were, in fact, writing the right book for the right audience, some interesting but not surprising results bubbled up. We found that some CISOs had concerns that the board wasn't 100% clear on the role of the CISO, or the role played by the security team. No matter who presents security messaging to the board, there are some things you should know (or make yourself aware of), and, therefore, some important questions to ask, such as:

- Who is *accountable* for keeping the organisation secure? (Given that, in most organisations at the time of writing, the board is ultimately *responsible* for keeping the organisation secure.)
- Who is leading the implementation of the strategy? (Even if it's part of the IT strategy.)
- Who has thought through the risks?

Throughout this book, we have used the term CISO, chief information security officer, as a blanket expression for security leadership. If your organisation does not have a CISO, it may be that management have assigned security-related activities to others – which is fine, as long as someone owns security and the messages that you receive as a board are unfiltered, transparent, and fact-based when it comes to cyber risk.

Chief information security officers

Formally, the role of a chief information security officer 'requires a combination of technical and soft skills, such as business acumen, leadership, communications and relationship building'.[59] We would also include risk management and assessment, general management skills, analytical skills, people leadership experience, a curious mind, and technical literacy. Our position on the technical nature of a CISO is that a strong technical literacy is required, but not all organisations need a CISO with a computer engineering degree or the ability to configure a firewall. Irrespective of their university degree, it is how they apply their knowledge, personal attributes, and business acumen that is important. The right CISO is one who can deliver against their objectives and provide the following:

- advice regarding protection of critical information assets
- ability to present and understand enterprise and cyber risks and their assessment
- strategic guidance
- coordinate alignment of cyber security and business initiatives
- oversee the cyber security team and broader operating model
- manage the security budget
- work with suppliers in relation to the ever growing third-party security risks
- act as a thought leader in security
- lead a cultural and behavioural security influence program
- oversee security-incident response activities
- brief the board, committees, executive and broad stakeholder community on cyber risk
- often, is the owner of one or a number of cyber risks, such as data loss
- interact with internal and external auditors and assess their requirements
- keep across industry-related risks, threats, and peer incidents
- oversee regulatory issues, requirements, and audits in relation to cyber

This list is by no means exhaustive. The items on this list also may not all be the responsibility of the CISO in your organisation. Security leaders take many shapes, forms, and titles. The bottom line is that every organisation needs the above responsibilities taken care of by someone, whether a start-up, a government department, or a 'mature' global organisation. Most organisations need to be able to point to a responsible officer, when it comes to security. Depending on the size and complexity of the business, this could be a network security leader who has strong business acumen and a supportive CIO. Or it could be a broader, maturing organisation that is ready for security leadership at the executive level, after a number of years of security being led by an IT security manager. Some organisations still need a tactical, technical resource to lead security. As long as someone is still responsible for the security strategy, vision, and standards to be upheld. It's ok for you to have a security team that is commensurate with your business operations and risk exposure.

Security maturity is an evolution. Young organisations tend to have an all-hands-on-deck approach, where the leader and the deliverers all sit within pitching distance of each other and there is a trust that is only gained through blood, sweat, and tears in their early forming days. As the business grows, governance and compliance (should) become more important to the business. As the need to protect your critical information assets is recognised, more formal security expertise should be sought. Initially, this may be in the shape of an advisor until an inhouse resource can be identified. The key to having security expertise is that it is contextual, timely, and relevant for the risk your organisation faces.

The hiring of a security leader and subsequent approval of a cyber security strategy is likely to see a need for a new operating model and increased team/capabilities. It is unlikely that the size of the team will ever reduce, given the increasing and changing nature of threats, regulatory demands, and general overwhelming workload involved in securing an organisation. While contractors are needed now and then for specific programs of work, the day-to-day operations of a security team almost always requires permanent security professionals who hold the history of cyber in their minds, but, more importantly, have the trust of their peers across the business – valuable IP. The value of having a permanent security team who are challenged, passionate, and have important, relevant work to complete can be the difference between success and failure of your security objectives. With a skills shortage and talent crisis in the security market, retention is key, not just of your CISO but of all the professionals in your security organisation.

The CISO may not be the only accountable or responsible party when it comes to cyber risk, but they need to be able to provide you with a risk view across the enterprise. We talked earlier about how the first time you meet the CISO should not be during a crisis. Their role isn't just firefighting. It is leading the security team, the enterprise, and, indeed, the board when it comes to cyber risk, strategy, finance and culture – four areas that are not dissimilar to the areas that a board is keenly focussed on for the rest of the enterprise.

Hiring and retaining a CISO or equivalent

A key risk to your security strategy and overall business operations is attrition. Hiring and retaining security leaders has become more and more challenging in recent years. These roles can sit empty for months, as recruitment efforts wane. This occurs because it is often found that in sourcing candidates for security leadership positions (and other security roles), hiring managers seek a combination of expertise, experience, and skill that does not exist in the one professional.

A lack of security leadership – and succession, for that matter – can increase risk to your organisation. Once a CISO builds trust and rapport across the executive, board, and sub-committees, the impact of the CISO leaving can be great. Having said that, everyone is (and should be) replaceable; businesses and boards must recognise that the CISO may need to change as the organisation's risk profile or regulatory requirements change. The skill set required to manage cyber risk for your organisation will evolve.

Boards may need to consider retention bonuses (not just financial), as well as making sure the organisation has hired the right leader in the first place. This may seem like an operational decision for the CIO to make, but the board may not feel like the right choice has been made – they may need to be educated as to why that particular CISO was chosen. As mentioned in the previous element, if you find yourself wanting to hear from the CIO more often than the CISO on security matters, maybe you haven't got the right CISO, or their skills need uplifting.

Trust

Establishing trust between you and your CISO is key to ensuring that security risk is within appetite and can be managed appropriately. Without this trust, it will be difficult for you to endorse any ask from the CISO, and for the CISO to feel heard by the board, in terms of their broader decision making.

'When the Board trusts the CISO, the CISO can do better, move quicker, act in the way they need to and get the funds they need. That's critical, because cyber security risk is so dynamic. It requires CISOs to adjust the strategy and operating model very quickly. And if the CISO doesn't have the support of management and the Board, he or she can't do their job', says Kris Lovejoy, the global cyber security leader at professional services firm Ernst & Young.[60]

It is the security leader's role to make sure that the security strategy consistently aligns to the business direction, all the while ensuring that risks and threats are managed. This could mean refreshing the strategy annually, updating the security outsource partners used, or providing additional assurance to auditors or regulators. With mutual trust, they will bring forward transparent, legally discoverable board papers for discussion or resolution in partnership with you. This may sound like a utopia. If you are starting from a zero base, mutual trust and transparency between the board and the CISO is a strong starting point.

Key lessons and reflections

We mentioned earlier in the book that a CISO, alone, cannot achieve all the security demands of an organisation. As a director, there are parts of the security leadership, culture, strategy, and risk that fall upon you to care for. These certainly include displaying behaviours that are security conscious, applying a security lens to all programs and decisions making that the board are responsible for, and working with the regulator on matters of cyber security. Your ability to execute your fiduciary responsibilities relies a lot on the information provided to you by your CISO and other executives. The role the CISO plays in educating the board and management is essential, and this role cannot be successful if the professional chosen as the CISO does not have the trust, rapport, and capabilities needed to lead the protection of your environment.

Areas for reflection

- What process was followed to hire our CISO? If an internal hire was chosen and we provided a step up for a less experienced security professional, how are we ensuring that appropriate leadership and strategy capabilities and skills are available? Furthermore, if an internal hire was selected, are we sure they meet all the non-negotiable criteria required in selecting a CISO? If an external hire was sourced, what key criteria for the role went to market to ensure we have a CISO who can work within the context and risk position of this organisation?
- Do I trust the CISO and CIO in their assessment of our cyber security position? What can I do to feel more comfortable?

Questions to ask during a board meeting

- If we do not have a CISO, who is accountable for security in our organisation?
- What is the succession plan for the CISO?
- What does the CISO need from the board?
- What is keeping the CISO awake at night?

CONTINOUS LEARNING FOR GOVERNING CYBER RISK

'When it comes to cybersecurity, the board needs to acknowledge that the organisation will constantly deal with dilemmas filled with ambiguity. As an example, we want our customers to contact us and engage digitally while we also want to protect the organisation from cyber risk. As a board member, holding the executive leadership accountable for integrating systems that productively deal with this ambiguity, is the greatest leverage point the board has to mitigate risks of all kind.'

Tim Banner, Partner, Reconceive Consulting Pty Ltd

By this point of the book, our aim is that you feel informed and a little hungry for more information in relation to cyber. Regrettably, it is not possible to provide you with the assurance of everything that needs to be in place to keep an organisation safe from a cyber attack. This global challenge is far more complex than that. However, through the elements of this book, you now understand the complexity and emerging risk surrounding cyber security. This book, and the topics covered, were thoughtfully designed to provide a holistic, high-level perspective of the areas of cyber security for you to explore, challenge, and monitor.

When it comes to cyber security, an educated board provide improvements in the board process, which can lead to a big freeing up of executive time. Ultimately, this can only benefit the business in the long run. At the end of the day, as directors, you already know you need to have a strong understanding of risk to meet your fiduciary responsibilities. And cyber risk is no different. What we have shared with you are some fundamentals to whet your appetite. We want you to continue learning from this starting point.

1. If you can demonstrate a risk-based approach to governance, you are 70% there. Ideally, the elements we outline can and will continue to guide you through the other 30%. That deeper knowledge of cyber security is a need for all directors in the same way that you must know about the organisation's financials, solvency, governance, reputation, and the law as it pertains to the business you are in.

2. Our aim was that, with your newfound knowledge, your confidence to ask questions and understand the answers has grown. Your desire to raise cyber as a conversation worth having has also grown, and the importance of your relationship with your security leadership is clear.

3. Your confidence in the cyber security posture of your organisation must stretch from before, to during and to after an incident. Resilience is a much wiser goal than zero tolerance. With your brand intact and a transparent approach to incident response within your organisation, this preparation will set you apart from dozens of peers in your industry.

4. The cyber security strategy is equally important for the board, regulators, the organisation, and the cyber security team. It provides strategic direction and clear objectives. Cyber security strategies vary, based on the organisation. Often, the implementation of the strategy is sequenced in order of addressing significant threats – these decisions are trade-offs. The implementation roadmap will adapt as emerging threats come to life. Your understanding and engagement with security leadership, and challenge to gain comfort in these

trade-offs, is important to your fiduciary commitments and to your relationship with management.

5. As the saying of the well-known management thinker Peter Drucker goes, you can't manage what you don't measure. When presented with metrics by your CISO, remember to read between the lines. There are insights to be had. The key is to ensure the metrics you receive are maturing as the business matures.

This book is not all you need to know about cyber

While serving on any board, at any time you can pick up this book and read one element as a refresher for board agenda items. Each gives you tips on questions to ask and relevant information, no matter what the CISO brings to you for decision making, noting, or discussion.

Being well informed doesn't mean you know all there is to know about cyber. More than anything, cyber changes daily. Our objective in writing this for you was to demonstrate that cyber security principles for boards can be learned, embraced, and instil confidence. You don't need to be a technology expert. You do need to know why cyber is important, how to address cyber risk, and understand the marriage of threats with impact in relation to your risk position.

With this book in hand, you can refer to the suggested questions at the end of each element to support your thinking. Moreover, you should also feel confident to seek out further support at the right time, such as from an independent advisor, as long as this is supplementary to your time with the CIO and/or CISO. It may be that the CISO is too close to the project or strategy and that a second set of eyes will help to break down any concepts you are not comfortable with. Overall, to sign off the strategy or any security program, you must feel a level of comfort and confidence and the source of this informed feeling can be numerous.

Next steps

Our advice from here on in is to keep learning. To both discharge your duties and be an effective participant in boardroom cyber conversations, stay across cyber activities in the public domain, but also stay across the opinions of your inhouse cyber leaders. Your relationship with the CISO cannot be understated. The best way to do this is to have a curious mind. Approach cyber in the same way you approach understanding other expectations of a director. You wouldn't attest to the financial situation of a business if you didn't fully understand the numbers, so aim to obtain a fluency in cyber to an appropriate level.

Many directors are on numerous boards and this can both help and hinder the process of understanding cyber risk. By all means, reflect on what other organisations are doing in relation to cyber across your board portfolio. Also, take a principles approach to your cyber thinking, as each organisation is unique in their cyber risk appetite, controls, and threat exposure.

For those of you who enjoy a wide variety of information sources, there are podcasts, books, publications, and events that can help you to understand this topic further. We have placed a list on our website (current at the time of writing) for you to explore.

Emerging trends

We don't believe anyone could have predicted that, in 2020, all or most board meetings (at least in some states and territories of Australia) would be conducted via Zoom. That, as a director, your technical skills would be stretched to keep pace with COVID-19. But other changes in 2020 have been just as significant for boards when it comes to cyber. The Australian Cyber Security Strategy 2020 was published that has all the hallmarks of a change in directors' duties when it comes to cyber. Artificial Intelligence (AI) is gaining ground on being aligned to a human brain, and David Attenborough let us know that if we don't stop some of our habits now, there will be no planet in 80 years' time. These are some pretty significant trends that the board cannot ignore. Simply querying the legal, financial and reputational risks of these global trends may no longer be enough. Five years ago, APRA didn't have CPS234, there were no modern slavery laws, and even climate change was still growing in importance. There is no hiding from the impact – financial, reputational, and legal – from these trends. Cyber is no different.

One final thought

If, as you finish this book, you pop it into your carry-on luggage, put it on your bookshelf, or place it on your night stand, and you sigh and then carry on with your day, seeing no further action to be taken, we ask one thing of you:

Imagine that your organisation is coming through its first major cyber incident. What have you learnt? What do you wish had been done differently? What do you wish you had known or thought of?

Through a post-incident mindset, you can change the lens through which you see the world. We encourage you to take a post-incident mindset to the matters before you – not fearful, but curious. Be bold in your thinking about every ask of the board: *What could be the cyber impact of these decisions before us?* And, finally, not all cyber is daunting. Your growing knowledge from this book, and your broader reading, will assist to allay concerns and form new questions in your mind, the answers to which will build your confidence as to whether your organisation is cyber safe.

Endnotes

1 'Daniels v Anderson (1995) 37 NSWLR 438', Law Case Summaries, accessed October 19, 2020, https://lawcasesummaries.com/knowledge-base/daniels-v-anderson-1995-37-nswlr-438/.

2 Re City Equitable Fire Insurance Co, Wikipedia, accessed October 19, 2020, https://en.wikipedia.org/wiki/Re_City_Equitable_Fire_Insurance_Co.

3 James Shipton, 'Launch of ASIC's report on director and officer oversight of non-financial risk', Transcript of a keynote address at the Australian Institute of Company Directors, Essential Director Update, Sydney, 2 October 2019, https://asic.gov.au/about-asic/news-centre/speeches/launch-of-asic-s-report-on-director-and-officer-oversight-of-non-financial-risk/.

4 *Corporations Act 2001*, C2018C00031, No. 50, 2001, Section 5.3, Federal Register of Legislation, 1 January 2018, https://www.legislation.gov.au/Details/C2018C00031

5 'Glossary 'C'', Australian Government, Australian Signals Directorate, Australian Cyber Security Centre. Accessed October 19, 2020, https://www.cyber.gov.au/acsc/view-all-content/glossary/c.

6 'Glossary 'C'', Australian Cyber Security Centre.

7 Alastair MacGibbon, 'Recent cyber attacks just the tip of the iceberg for Australia', *The Australian Financial Review*, May 18, 2020, https://www.afr.com/technology/recent-cyber-attacks-just-the-tip-of-the-iceberg-for-australia-20200515-p54thf.

8 Jason Choi, Harrison Lung, and James Kaplan, 'A framework for improving cybersecurity discussions within organizations', *McKinsey Digital*, November 10, 2017, https://assets.mckinsey.com/business-functions/mckinsey-digital/our-insights/a-framework-for-improving-cybersecurity-discussions-within-organizations.

9 Barbara Burgess, 'Businesses consider cybersecurity as an afterthought despite growth in attacks, EY survey finds', Ernst & Young Press Release, 18 February 2020, London, GB, https://www.ey.com/en_gl/news/2020/02/businesses-consider-cybersecurity-as-an-afterthought-despite-growth-in-attacks-ey-survey-finds.

10 World Economic Forum, 'The Global Risks Landscape 2020 Survey Results: What is the impact and likelihood of technological risks?', accessed October 19, 2020, http://reports.weforum.org/global-risks-report-2020/survey-results/global-risks-landscape-2020/#landscape///technological. Survey respondents were asked to assess the likelihood of the individual

global risk on a scale of 1 to 5, with 1 representing a very unlikely risk, and 5 representing a very likely risk. They also assessed the impact of each global risk on a scale of 1 to 5, with 1 representing a minimal impact and 5 a catastrophic impact.

11 Beverley Head, 'What boards can do in the event of a cyber breach', Australian Institute of Company Directors, October 01, 2019, https://aicd. companydirectors.com.au/membership/company-director-magazine/2019-back-editions/october/cyber-breaches.

12 Nadia Cameron, 'Rachel Botsman: Trust is the currency of the 21st Century', CMO from IDG, July 29, 2015, https://www.cmo.com.au/article/580694/rachel-botsman-trust-new-currency-21st-century/.

13 Michelle Drolet, '5 cybersecurity events that keep CEOs up at night', October 26, 2020, https://www.propertycasualty360.com/2020/10/26/5-cybersecurity-events-that-keep-ceos-up-at-night.

14 University of Kent (Dan Worth), 'At least 57 negative impacts from cyber-attacks', *Science Daily*, October 24, 2018, https://www.sciencedaily.com/releases/2018/10/181024112203.htm.

15 Louis Columbus, 'CIO's Guide to Stopping Privileged Access Abuse – Part 2', April 25, 2019, https://www.forbes.com/sites/louiscolumbus/2019/04/25/cios-guide-to-stopping-privileged-access-abuse-part-2.

16 Samantha Schwartz, '"Rogue" employees caused Shopify's data breach. What makes an insider a threat?', *CIO Dive*, September 24, 2020, https://www.ciodive.com/news/shopify-breach-security-insider-forrester/585823/.

17 Blake Morgan, '100 Stats on Digital Transformation and Customer Experience', December 16, 2019, https://www.forbes.com/sites/blakemorgan/2019/12/16/100-stats-on-digital-transformation-and-customer-experience.

18 Michelle Drolet, '5 cybersecurity events that keep CEOs up at night', October 26, 2020, https://www.propertycasualty360.com/2020/10/26/5-cybersecurity-events-that-keep-ceos-up-at-night.

19 Jim Schleckser, 'Using Stories and Symbols to Build a Powerful Culture', January 27, 2015, https://www.inc.com/jim-schleckser/use-stories-and-symbols-to-build-a-powerful-culture.html.

20 Maria Gourtsilidou, 'Top 10 Threats That CEOs Are Concerned In 2020', *CEOWorld Magazine*, May 4, 2020, https://ceoworld.biz/2020/05/04/top-10-threats-that-ceos-are-concerned-in-2020/.

21 Nick Galletto, Timothy Murphy, Ed Powers, 'Cyber, cyber everywhere', *Deloitte Insights*, July 29, 2019, https://www2.deloitte.com/global/en/insights/topics/risk-management/cyber-security-threats.html.

22 'What is a notifiable data breach?', Australian Government, Office of the Australian Information Commissioner, accessed November 4, 2020, https://www.oaic.gov.au/privacy/data-breaches/what-is-a-notifiable-

data-breach/#:~:text=Under%20the%20Notifiable%20Data%20
Breaches,financial%20loss%20through%20fraud.

23 'How to Explain the Equifax Breach? Start with the Culture', School of
Continuing Studies, News & Events, Georgetown University, September
15, 2017, https://scs.georgetown.edu/news-and-events/article/6646/how-
explain-equifax-breach-start-culture.

24 Hatch, M.J. (1993). 'The dynamics of organizational culture', The Academy
of Management Review 18, pp. 657–693, as referenced in Kine Reegård,
Claire Blackett & Vikash Katta, 'The Concept of Cybersecurity Culture',
conference paper, 29th European Safety and Reliability Conference
(ESREL) At: Hannover, September 2019. https://www.researchgate.net/
publication/336149766_The_Concept_of_Cybersecurity_Culture.

25 Reegård, Blackett & Katta, 'The Concept of Cybersecurity Culture'.

26 'Cost of a Data Breach Report 2020', IBM Security, Cost of a Data Breach
Report 2020, accessed November 30, 2020, https://www.ibm.com/security/
digital-assets/cost-data-breach-report/#/.

27 'Cost of a Data Breach Report 2020', IBM Security.

28 Filip Truta, 'Businesses Can Lose Half of Customers After a Data Breach,
Research Shows', Bitdefender Business Insights Blog, September 20, 2019, https://
businessinsights.bitdefender.com/businesses-can-lose-up-to-58-of-customers-after-
a-data-breach-research-shows#:~:text=Businesses%20Can%20Lose%20Half%20
of%20Customers%20after%20a%20Data%20Breach%2C%20Research%20
Shows,-By%20Filip%20Truta&text=For%20example%2C%2083%25%20
of%20consumers,never%20return%20to%20that%20business.

29 'Australian Red Cross Blood Service data breach', Australian Government,
Office of the Australian Information Commissioner, News and Media,
August 7, 2017, https://www.oaic.gov.au/updates/news-and-media/
australian-red-cross-blood-service-data-breach/.

30 Stephanie Palmer-Derrien, 'Marketing fluff: What startups can learn from Canva's
data-breach response', www.smartcompany.com.au, May 27, 2019, https://www.
smartcompany.com.au/startupsmart/analysis/canva-data-breach-response/.

31 'Cyber security: the role of boards', KPMG Insights, April 20, 2017, https://
home.kpmg/au/en/home/insights/2017/04/cyber-security-role-of-boards.
html.

32 'Building a practical cybersecurity risk acceptance/risk transfer framework',
accessed November 30, 2020, https://www.bakertilly.com/insights/building-
a-practical-cybersecurity-risk-acceptance-risk-transfer-framework/.

33 Aaron Steele, 'Are you cyber resilient?', October 31, 2019, http://wbn.
co.nz/2019/10/31/are-you-cyber-resilient/.

34 'Businesses in the dark: McAfee survey reveals disconnect in cybersecurity
culture and cyber resilience', Australian Cyber Security Magazine, January 28,
2020, https://australiancybersecuritymagazine.com.au/businesses-in-the-

dark-mcafee-survey-reveals-disconnect-in-cybersecurity-culture-and-cyber-resilience/.

35 'How to Develop a Cyber Security Strategy at the Board Level', https://consciousgovernance.com/, accessed November 30, 2020, \https://consciousgovernance.com/blog-archives/how-to-develop-a-cyber-security-strategy-at-the-board-level.

36 Christopher Wray, 'The FBI and Corporate Directors: Working Together to Keep Companies Safe from Cyber Crime', October 1, 2018, https://www.fbi.gov/news/speeches/the-fbi-and-corporate-directors-working-together-to-keep-companies-safe-from-cyber-crime.

37 Australian Stock Exchange 'ASX Cyber Health Check Report', April 2017, https://www.asx.com.au/documents/investor-relations/ASX-100-Cyber-Health-Check-Report.pdf.

38 'Major Third-party Data Breaches Revealed in March 2020', April 3, 2020, https://normshield.com/major-third-party-data-breaches-revealed-in-march-2020/.

39 Ry Crozier, 'WA Health traces data leak to third-party pager service', July 21, 2020, https://www.itnews.com.au/news/wa-health-traces-data-leak-to-third-party-pager-service-550679.

40 Alyse Stanley, 'Amazon Employees Leak Customer Data To Third-Party Agent (Again)', January 11, 2020, https://www.gizmodo.com.au/2020/01/amazon-employees-leak-customer-data-to-third-party-agent-again/.

41 Patrick Kehoe, '3 Tips For Successfully Running Tech Outside the IT Department', November 11, 2020, https://www.darkreading.com/operations/3-tips-for-successfully-running-tech-outside-the-it-department/a/d-id/1339245.

42 Stefan Deutscher, 'Five Ways Business Directors Can Prepare for the Future of Cybersecurity', *Forbes Magazine Online*, World Economic Forum Contributor, January 5, 2020, https://www.forbes.com/sites/worldeconomicforum/2020/01/15/five-ways-business-directors-can-prepare-for-the-future-of-cybersecurity/#64f942516b58.

43 'Businesses in the dark: McAfee survey reveals disconnect in cybersecurity culture and cyber resilience' *Australian Cyber Security Magazine*, January 28, 2020, https://australiancybersecuritymagazine.com.au/businesses-in-the-dark-mcafee-survey-reveals-disconnect-in-cybersecurity-culture-and-cyber-resilience/.

44 'How much would a data breach cost your business', IBM, accessed November 30, 2020, https://www.ibm.com/security/data-breach.

45 'Businesses in the dark: McAfee survey reveals disconnect in cybersecurity culture and cyber resilience', *Australian Cyber Security Magazine*, January 28, 2020, https://australiancybersecuritymagazine.com.au/businesses-in-the-dark-mcafee-survey-reveals-disconnect-in-cybersecurity-culture-and-cyber-resilience/.

46 Lance Spitzner, 'This Is Why the Human Is the Weakest Link', Sans Security Awareness, accessed November 30, 2020, https://www.sans.org/security-awareness-training/blog/why-human-weakest-link.

47 Steve Morgan, 'Cybercrime to Cost the World $10.5 Trillion Annually By 2025', *Cybercrime Magazine*, November 13, 2020, https://cybersecurityventures.com/hackerpocalypse-cybercrime-report-2016/.

48 'Cost of a Data Breach Report 2020', IBM Security, Cost of a Data Breach Report 2020, accessed November 30, 2020, https://www.ibm.com/security/digital-assets/cost-data-breach-report/#/.

49 Justin Flower, '"Be prepared and be brave": The Salvos reveal how they prepare for cyber attack', November 9, 2020, https://probonoaustralia.com.au/news/2020/11/be-prepared-and-be-brave-the-salvos-reveal-how-they-prepare-for-cyber-attack/.

50 Australian Prudential Regulatory Authority, 'Prudential Standard CPS 234 Information Security', July 2019, https://www.apra.gov.au/sites/default/files/cps_234_july_2019_for_public_release.pdf.

51 'Cost of a Data Breach Report 2020', IBM, https://www.ibm.com/security/digital-assets/cost-data-breach-report/#/.

52 Jessica Stillman, 'Steve Jobs Knew Success Was All About Saying No. This Mental Trick Will Make You Much Better at It', February 17, 2020, https://www.inc.com/jessica-stillman/when-to-say-no-mental-trick.html.

53 Julie Bernard & Mark Nicholson, 'Reshaping the cybersecurity landscape', *Deloitte Insights*, July 24, 2020, https://www2.deloitte.com/us/en/insights/industry/financial-services/cybersecurity-maturity-financial-institutions-cyber-risk.html.

54 Jason Choi, Harrison Lung, and James Kaplan, 'A framework for improving cybersecurity discussions within organizations', *McKinsey Digital*, November 10, 2017, https://assets.mckinsey.com/business-functions/mckinsey-digital/our-insights/a-framework-for-improving-cybersecurity-discussions-within-organizations#.

55 Dr Catherina Richter, 'Cyber insurance claims on the rise', Helpnet Cyber Security, November 27, 2020, https://www.helpnetsecurity.com/2020/11/27/cyber-insurance-claims-rise/.

56 Julie Bernard & Mark Nicholson, 'Reshaping the cybersecurity landscape', *Deloitte Insights*, July 24, 2020, https://www2.deloitte.com/us/en/insights/industry/financial-services/cybersecurity-maturity-financial-institutions-cyber-risk.html.

57 Jason Choi, Harrison Lung, and James Kaplan, 'A framework for improving cybersecurity discussions within organizations', *McKinsey Digital*, November 10, 2017, https://assets.mckinsey.com/business-functions/mckinsey-digital/our-insights/a-framework-for-improving-cybersecurity-discussions-within-organizations#.

58 'How much would a data breach cost your business?', IBM, accessed November 30, 2020, https://www.ibm.com/security/data-breach.

59 'Guidance for Cyber Security Roles – Chief Information Security Officer', Australian Government, Australian Signals Directorate, Australian Cyber Security Centre. Accessed December 2, 2020, https://www.cyber.gov.au/acsc/view-all-content/guidance/chief-information-security-officer.

60 Mary K. Pratt, '4 signs the CISO-board relationship is broken (and 3 ways to fix it)', July 18, 2019, https://www.csoonline.com/article/3406444/4-signs-the-ciso-board-relationship-is-broken-and-3-ways-to-fix-it.html.